Praise for *Don't Settle for Safe*

If you've ever sensed there could be more for you in life, this book is the missing clue. Although Sarah J. Roberts is my daughter, I can honestly say that she is one of the most courageous people I have ever met. Her amazing book shows us the power and reward that makes the daring faith life worth the risk!

Playing it safe makes winning an impossibility. The Bible is full of men and women who forsook the safety of the comfortable for the unsettling place that leads to the satisfaction of accomplishing our God-given purpose. Sarah draws from ancient and contemporary examples to beat the drum strongly in this book.

She rallies the believer to come out of the trenches. It's an exhilarating experience to read it, and an amazing adventure to watch these principles change your life. This is a must-read! If you're going anywhere in life, don't leave home without it.

—Bishop T.D. Jakes, #1 *New York Times* bestselling author
and senior pastor of The Potter's House in Dallas, Texas

Sarah Jakes Roberts is living proof that living a daring and bold life can be incredibly transformative. In *Don't Settle for Safe* she uses the depths of her experiences as a deep well of transparency to help those in need find relief from their pain. This book will help you discover how to use the most uncomfortable moments in your life as fuel to unleash the unstoppable power that lies within you.

—DeVon Franklin and Meagan Good, *New York Times* bestselling authors of *The Wait*

Sarah Jakes Roberts is brilliantly honest and open, making us ask out loud the questions we've all had inside at some point. She eloquently challenges us to be bold and to love God out loud with no fear. This book will bless and transform many lives.

—Erica Campbell, contemporary R&B recording artist

The myth of safety and the pursuit of comfort and security has caused so many to miss the abundant, purpose-driven adventure that God has for us. Jesus did not come to earth, die on the cross, and rise again on the third day to make us safe. He came to make us dangerous to the kingdom of darkness. I'm so grateful for Sarah's voice in our generation. I love her engaging, honest, transparent, vulnerable, and passionate writing style. *Don't Settle for Safe* is a timely book that calls out the greatness in you. You will be inspired and equipped to live your one and only life wholeheartedly. God has so much more for you. Step out and take some risks. You can trust him.

—Christine Caine, author of *Unashamed* and founder of Propel

This book is not only a testament to God's love for us, it's also a guide offering practical advice to use in strengthening your personal relationship with God. I applaud Sarah's transparency in an effort to inspire and empower others.

—Cookie Johnson, wife to Magic Johnson

If you are ready to be open and honest with your feelings, identify your mistakes, and are ready to do the work needed to bring change in your life, this book will help you break everything that is holding you back. Sarah's willingness to be honest but gentle, in her way to correct you, is something I've never experienced before while reading a book. You will find yourself being who she describes; you'll even say things like "that's someone else I know; it's not me!" Thank you, Sarah, for encouraging us to be courageous and to never settle for safe.

—Michelle Williams, singer/songwriter

I am blown away by the wisdom, revelation, and transparency in *Don't Settle for Safe*. A must-read for every male and female who desires to experience the fullness of authentic God-given relationship.

—Nancy Alcorn, founder of Mercy Ministries and author
of *Ditch the Baggage, Change Your Life*

Don't Settle for Safe grabs you from the first line and never lets you go. Sarah's vulnerability and transparency allow the reader to experience every high and empathize with every low. Many times I found myself in tears as her inspiring and thought-provoking honesty challenged me to look within myself in compelling ways—something we all must do to experience true growth.

—Sanya Richards-Ross, Olympic gold-medal winner in track and field

Sarah is such a truly beautiful writer and a woman of great wisdom and bravery. Each chapter in this book is a hand reaching out, inviting you to be courageous enough to grow into the person God created you to be. I love it.

—Shauna Niequist, *New York Times* bestselling author of *Present over Perfect*

I wish I'd read this book when I was eighteen. Sarah has wisdom way beyond her years. She tells the truth with staggering vulnerability, for no other reason than her passionate mandate to help readers understand their value in Christ. For many, this will be a life-changing book.

—Sheila Walsh, cohost of *Life Today* and author of *The Longing in Me*

In this book, Sarah gets to the heart of most of our issues by reminding us that, regardless of what we've done and how we may feel about the paths our lives have taken, God still loves us. She masterfully yet gently, from the perspective of one having experienced life's tough spots, connects our belief in God's unfailing love to our success in cultivating love in our intimate relationships. I am so proud of the work that my friend Sarah is doing as she shares her life's lessons with the world. I believe that she is one of the greatest voices of our generation because she chooses daily to remain transparent in her quest to reach the broken.

—Tasha Cobbs, Grammy Award–winning artist

Don't Settle *for* Safe

Other Books by Sarah Jakes Roberts

Lost & Found
Colliding with Destiny
Dear Mary

Don't Settle *for* Safe

Embracing
the Uncomfortable
to Become
Unstoppable

SARAH JAKES ROBERTS

NELSON
BOOKS

An Imprint of Thomas Nelson

Published in Nashville, Tennessee, by Nelson Books, an imprint of Thomas Nelson. Nelson Books and Thomas Nelson are registered trademarks of HarperCollins Christian Publishing, Inc.

Thomas Nelson titles may be purchased in bulk for educational, business, fund-raising, or sales promotional use. For information, please e-mail SpecialMarkets@ThomasNelson.com.

Unless otherwise noted, Scripture quotations are taken from the New King James Version®. © 1982 by Thomas Nelson. Used by permission. All rights reserved.

Scripture quotations marked KJV are from the King James Version. Public domain.

Scripture quotations marked NIV are from the Holy Bible, New International Version®, NIV®. Copyright © 1973, 1978, 1984, 2011 by Biblica, Inc.™ Used by permission of Zondervan. All rights reserved worldwide. www.zondervan.com. The "NIV" and "New International Version" are trademarks registered in the United States Patent and Trademark Office by Biblica, Inc.™

Scripture quotations marked NLT are taken from the Holy Bible, New Living Translation. © 1996, 2004, 2007, 2013 by Tyndale House Foundation. Used by permission of Tyndale House Publishers, Inc., Carol Stream, Illinois 60188. All rights reserved.

Scripture quotations marked ESV are taken from the ESV® Bible (The Holy Bible, English Standard Version®). Copyright © 2001 by Crossway, a publishing ministry of Good News Publishers. Used by permission. All rights reserved.

Any Internet addresses, phone numbers, or company or product information printed in this book are offered as a resource and are not intended in any way to be or to imply an endorsement by Thomas Nelson, nor does Thomas Nelson vouch for the existence, content, or services of these sites, phone numbers, companies, or products beyond the life of this book.

ISBN 9780718081973 (eBook)

ISBN 9780718095888 (IE)

Library of Congress Cataloging-in-Publication Data

Names: Roberts, Sarah Jakes, 1988-author.
Title: Don't settle for safe: embracing the uncomfortable to become
    unstoppable / Sarah Jakes Roberts.
Description: Nashville, Tennessee: Nelson Books, an imprint of Thomas
    Nelson, [2017] | Includes bibliographical references.
Identifiers: LCCN 2016044240 | ISBN 9780718081966
Subjects: LCSH: Risk-taking (Psychology)—Religious aspects—Christianity. |
    Self-actualization (Psychology)—Religious aspects—Christianity.
Classification: LCC BV4598.15 .R63 2017 | DDC 248.4—dc23 LC record available at
https://lccn.loc.gov/2016044240

Printed in the United States of America

17 18 19 20 21 LSC 10 9 8 7 6 5 4 3

This book is dedicated to the One who continues to cause all things to work together for my good and to those hoping to believe He can do the same for them too.

Contents

Foreword

Fear not, for I have redeemed you;
I have called you by name, you are mine.
When you pass through the waters, I will be with you;
and through the rivers, they shall not overwhelm you;
when you walk through fire you shall not be burned,
and the flame shall not consume you.

ISAIAH 43:1–2 ESV

These poignant words of the prophet Isaiah do not promise us a way around, but a way through. It is not a question of *if* you pass through waters that would threaten to overwhelm or walk through flames that would seek to consume you . . . it is simply a matter of *when*.

Redemption does not guarantee us safety in this world; it is a promise that we will never walk alone.

When I was a younger woman I didn't understand this. I wanted to avoid confrontation, exposure, and struggles at all cost. I am so thankful that God saw beyond my fears and spoke to the very longings of my heart. You see, everything I wanted was on the other side of my fears, and the same is true for you. It is the very reason that every God-breathed promise is preceded with the admonishment of *Fear not*.

Sarah Jakes Roberts understands this journey. *Don't Settle for Safe* is a brave book in which Sarah weaves together her legacy of wisdom with personal life experiences. Each page will encourage you to leave the relative safety of the shore and dare to navigate the choppy, turbulent waters of life.

Because you are *His*, my friend, you must choose to leave behind the shores of uncertainty. You were created for deep waters and holy fire.

Ultimately, God is more concerned with our condition than our comfort. Dare to believe this is the very reason He has allowed some things to become uncomfortable in your life, and by doing so, He reveals your true condition. I am so thankful that you have chosen not to settle. Don't fear the struggle; let it strengthen you. Thank you, Sarah, for including my words in your charge.

LISA BEVERE
New York Times bestselling author of *Without Rival*,
Lioness Arising, and *Girls with Swords*

Introduction

I was twenty-three years old when I made the choice to file for divorce. It was one of the most challenging decisions of my life so far, but I knew without a doubt that my mental, emotional, and spiritual health hung in the balance. So I did the hard thing and reconciled myself to the fact that my marriage was not and would never be the romantic, happily-ever-after tale I'd hoped for. Then I reassessed and created a new vision for my life. What I wanted in life was comfort and stability. I'd go after that dream alone as a single mother of two.

I thought that life was about arriving at a destination where all things made sense and each day had perfect harmony. I know now that I was telling myself yet another fairy tale. A life of constant comfort and stability—without any fears or insecurity—simply does not exist for me or for anyone. My heart, mind, and soul were searching for a place in life that did not exist: comfort. So in spite of my best efforts, situations arose for me daily that made me uncomfortable. Sure, there was a vision in my mind of who I could become if I overcame my fears, but that vision was often blocked by the insecurities that filled my head. Small challenges like presenting new ideas in business meetings made me sweat and squirm. Conflicts and trials with my young children sometimes made me feel overwhelmed.

I can remember thinking, *If I can just get over this one thing, then everything else will be smooth sailing!* But like waves on the ocean, that "one thing" I was able to overcome was followed by yet another. So how do we keep from feeling as though we're drowning when life seems too much for us to handle? Your power to overcome is in your willingness to not just anticipate but embrace the unpredictability of life. Being afraid of the unknown does not keep it at bay.

Life's challenges promise us endless opportunities to reassess, reevaluate, and push beyond the boundaries of comfort over and over again.

Life's challenges promise us endless opportunities to reassess, reevaluate, and push beyond the boundaries of comfort over and over again. No one understands that more than I do. After all, I became a mother at age fourteen. Since then I've been on a journey that has taught me a lot about myself. For a while I allowed other people and circumstances to control my journey, conforming as best I could to the expectations I perceived from my family and social circle. Each attempt backfired on me in grand fashion.

That journey has taught me some lessons that I hope will help you. I hope this book will serve as your guide to transformational freedom that comes from sacrificing the notion of comfort.

Each minute that passes by is transforming you. Biologically, your hair begins to turn gray, and your skin and muscles begin making a slow, graceful dance into older age. This is the beautiful cycle of life.

On the inside, learning to change and control the way we think about what we've faced does not come so naturally. Even more challenging is having the heart to look toward the future with optimism. In fact, it takes great intentionality.

But what I learned is that God does not promise us smooth sailing. It has been said that still waters run deep, but that is only true for bodies of water that are confined to a certain space. The deepest waters, like oceans and seas, have constant waves and ripples that make them the opposite of still; they are the epitome of powerful. The ocean is a part of an ecosystem that is much larger than what the eye can see. The consistent waves of the ocean testify to the ocean's tremendous power. There is life springing forth from its depths and winds grazing the top of the water that creates an unstoppable current. What's marvelous to consider is that the same Source that created the ocean, filled it with life, and set it in rhythm, created you. You are as unstoppable and powerful as the ocean!

I trust there have been moments in life when you, too, have felt as though you were barely hanging on, when the waves threatened to pull you under. When insecurities filled your head with all of the reasons you should be afraid. I know that voice well! I've heard it many times throughout my own process. It says things like, *Don't do it! You can't handle what will come after this.*

Even as you read this book, that voice may begin to haunt you, trying to convince you that your life's destiny is not worth the struggle. In those moments you get to choose between staying on the comfort of land or daring to be like the deep, vast ocean that creates both fascination and fear. As you're reading this book, I will share with you some of the concerns that surfaced in my heart as I chose to dig deeper. Your surface may be different or more complicated than mine, but it's important that you recognize the necessity of that voice.

If voices of insecurity, doubt, and fear are not confronted, they will dictate your life. You cannot silence these voices or ignore them. Instead, make them your audience as you dare to defy the limitations of your past.

You've been given the gift of being on earth for a reason. Recognizing who you are and what you have to offer will help you realize that you do not have to be a slave to any preconceived idea of what your life must look like.

If voices of insecurity, doubt, and fear are not confronted, they will dictate your life.

There may be times when feeling this way actually scares you into shrinking, but you were not meant to cower and resign yourself to a routine or pattern that makes you just like everyone else. The vibrancy of your life is contingent on your ability to accept situations that isolated you and to learn and be empowered by your unique imprint. It's going to take work, and it's going to demand transparency and vulnerability. It's going to dig deep into the areas of your life you've probably never examined before. It might not feel safe, but one thing is for sure. You will be transformed into a newer, better version of yourself. Let's get started!

1

No More Excuses

I am stuck in the persona I've created. But how can I dig deep when it's taking all that I have to hold myself together? Thinking of all the broken pieces scattered around my life makes me afraid to face tomorrow. But I long for freedom. I want to find the light that leads me out of this cave. Please, God, if You can see me, send me a reminder that You're still with me.

This is the moment that will change your life forever. You are finally becoming the person you always knew you could be. I wish I could say it's because you opened this book, but it's much bigger than that. You have decided it's time for you to be free. You've stopped trying to construct a life you hope other people will accept, and instead you've decided to embrace the life that God has in store for you. Nothing has happened to you that God can't use to restore you. The first step in that restoration is recognizing the power you've always had to pull yourself out of darkness and constantly push toward the light at the end of the tunnel.

Many times you felt like quitting, but you didn't. Maybe you were unhappy with the present, unsure about tomorrow, and too afraid to confront the past. Maybe, like me, you've thought, *If only I hadn't expected so much, then the pain wouldn't have been so great.* You've wondered if you should lower your expectations. One of life's greatest tests is resisting the urge to cave in to the pressure of that kind of frustration. And you've resisted. You're still dreaming big.

Despite the many tears that threatened to dilute it, your faith did not dissolve. Your heart is still pumping. Your pulse is a sign that this world needs you. All of your achievements, confusion, accolades, issues, awards, and pain prepared you for the journey. You know you were made for so much more than this.

Long before you became aware that life could be more bitter than sweet, you believed that nothing was impossible. The success of this book relies on you connecting with every part of you, especially the pieces that have been buried behind a smile. I want to speak to that purest, most innocent version of you. I want to speak to the child who once believed she could jump off of her bed and fly. I want to speak to the person who was so afraid of the dark that she needed her door cracked to let in a glimmer of light. Remember how you laughed without fear of how your joy would sound to other people and cried without concern that other people would think you were weak? You were fully alive. You felt everything and didn't need anything to numb you from your reality.

I hate that you've adjusted to the pain. Maybe, like me, you grew to a place where you hid your feelings, perhaps even from yourself. But as much as I might wish away the hurts that changed you, the truth is that those hurts created some of the most beautiful parts of your heart. That's right! You are armed with more wisdom, discernment, awareness, confidence, and joy than the innocent and delicate person you once were.

My mission is to open your eyes and help you see that longing for the past is an illusion. Your present holds more promise than anything that used to be. The cost of that vision is also the reward: transparency, vulnerability, and intimacy with God. At times you may be so uncomfortable you'll close this book, but you won't keep it closed for long. You know why? Your soul is begging for you to leave a door cracked open so that light can shine through.

You are armed with more wisdom, discernment, awareness, confidence, and joy than the innocent and delicate person you once were.

This is your season of change and transformation—your opportunity to grow. You are only as free as your mind will allow you to be. Taking control of your life will require you to be proactive, not reactive. But the power of this book cannot be unlocked unless it is read with an open heart and mind. For positive change to take place within your soul, no area can be off limits for examination. Daddy issues, mommy problems, sibling rivalry, low self-esteem, ambition without character, and fragile integrity are just a few of the areas we will explore. It won't be easy, but it will be worth it. You are worth it.

Growth is produced through sacrifice. It requires that you release the comfort of your last phase and learn the distinctions of the new one.

Clothes That Don't Fit Anymore

My husband and I have a blended family with six beautiful children. Touré had his three angels and I had my two. We were content with our small tribe, but as our love began to overflow, we began to dream of adding one more. And then came our baby girl, Ella.

When we were expecting our daughter, the doctor estimated that she'd be a little over eight pounds at time of birth. I didn't buy many newborn clothes because I know from experience how quickly babies grow. Ella surprised us all when she was born weighing just six pounds. So I quickly stocked up on tiny clothes and diapers. But just a few weeks later, Ella was two months old and already weighed twelve pounds. The slew of newborn diapers and clothes we'd acquired were no longer useful and needed to be given away. Luckily, she was too young to have any attachments to them.

Unfortunately, things were a bit more difficult for her six-year-old sister. When it became evident that Makenzie was outgrowing her clothes, I bought new ones, but I had to undertake a covert mission to get rid of what no longer fit. Even though the old clothes had grown uncomfortable, the nostalgic connection she had to them was strong. She refused to let go of them even though they were no longer useful.

It will take some time before she realizes that it's foolish to keep clothes that don't fit. She has yet to learn that the gift of growing requires letting go. We have to let go or we'll experience discomfort and even pain.

By now you know I'm not just talking about clothes.

Letting go is trusting that we can carry the lessons from our past in our hearts without constantly replaying the pain in our heads. You're likely much older than Makenzie, but I'm willing to go out on a limb and guess that there are some people, things, and ideas, or maybe patterns or behaviors in your life you've grown so accustomed to that the mere thought of confronting and separating from them gives you anxiety.

Trust me, I've been there!

Youthful Ambitions

So what is it in your life that you might need to let go of?

When I close my eyes, I can clearly see two extremely different versions of me. Neither are full expressions of who I am, but both are true. On one side I see a young, insecure girl pretending she's okay. A smile is plastered on her face, but it's more of a mask than a genuine expression. The sadness in her eyes betrays her. I see how lost her soul has become. Questions plague her and fears haunt her. She doesn't yet know her incredible potential. She doesn't know that even with her flaws and struggles, she is full of possibilities. She's not looking for an opportunity to catapult her to unprecedented heights; she's just looking for enough stability to feel "normal."

Then there's the other image. She has blossomed into her womanhood. She has learned that stability can only be attained through facing insecurities. She is no longer searching for an opportunity because she recognizes that there are too many to choose from already. She is content to chase God's destiny for her life. She understands that flaws are a necessary part of life because they foster humility. She has become a student of life and a teacher to all who will listen. Her heart has become perfectly aligned with a Source much stronger than her own will. She has met God and He has shown her the power in being her authentic self.

Both of these are versions of myself, but neither of them could exist without the other. The mystery for most of us is learning how to channel our insecurities into the empowerment necessary to maximize adulthood.

Is What You Wanted Then What You Need Now?

Stop for a minute and think about your own two selves—your young self and the one you want to be. Becoming who you want to be may demand that you get rid of old ideas about what success looks like. For me, this meant getting rid of the white-picket-fence illusion.

The presence of adolescent fears existing simultaneously with adult ambition is not isolated to the journey of womanhood. The same paradox exists for our male counterparts. From boyhood, men pride themselves on their ability to be rough and tough. When water begins to form in their eyes, we tell them to suck it up and that boys don't cry. Their youthful charm and boyish features earn them nicknames meant to be endearing, such as "heartbreaker" or "ladies' man." When we create a culture that congratulates men on their ability to hide their emotions, juggle multiple relationships, and resist vulnerability, we run the risk of producing men who internalize their fears and who break hearts rather than protect them. They, too, must learn to shed the behavior of their insecurities and trust themselves without the validation that comes from having a muscular build, dry eyes, and notches in their belts. How do you become a man of character and integrity when all you've heard is the applause that comes with indiscretions? Life brings us all to a fork in the road when we must choose to grow up into the unknown or grow cold by staying the same.

All throughout childhood, boys and girls are inundated with images of success. The most popular narrative painted a picture of a demure, educated, well-dressed, and well-behaved woman who captured the attention and heart of a powerful man. That man, through love and devotion, provided a comfortable life and a home bordered by the proverbial white picket fence. And they lived happily ever after.

Some of us followed the socially accepted trajectory toward such "success." It didn't take long, however, before we realized that even the modest goals of high school, college, career, marriage, home, and family take a lot of work. Unexpected events often delay or detour our desired accomplishments, and we begin to see that this thing called life requires an uncanny resolve to maintain peace in the middle of the raging storms. So what happens when, on our journey toward obtaining the white-picket-fence ideal, we lose touch with ourselves?

For me, the white picket fence represents the illusion of safety and normalcy that keeps us from facing the issues we've tucked away in our hearts. Of course hiding from our human frailty comes in all different shapes, sizes, and packages. Some of us swear off the notion of love altogether, others hide behind successful careers, and many feign an enjoyment and exhilaration that comes from being unchained to real morals or convictions. The bottom line is you'll never know who you can become if you create a life that requires you to pretend you're already comfortable with who you are.

Dangerous Comparison Game

Occasionally, we get a glimpse of how much our covetous perception of other people's lives was shaped by a very limited perspective. We knew our best friend wasn't perfect, but we never guessed she had a secret addiction. We were thinking our neighbors had it all together and then we learned their marriage was just as broken as ours. Our coworker with the most enviable house in town goes bankrupt. We learn that no one has life completely figured out and everyone is a little bit broken.

But mediocrity is comforting until it becomes debilitating. Witnessing dysfunction in other people's lives may make us more comfortable with our own, but this dangerous knowledge can also strip us of the motivation required to pursue a deeper level of self-intimacy and transformation.

You cannot point the finger at other people's shortcomings to justify your own. God doesn't grade our lives on a curve. He's given each of us a certain measure of faith and power to have an incredible life. Each of us has an opportunity to dust off the shame, fear, and pain that threatened to bury us and reemerge with strength and tenacity.

Resist the Urge to Lower Your Expectations

Moving on takes effort, intentionality, and discipline. If you're going to gather the broken pieces of your life and build again, you must be willing to clear your heart and mind of excuses. Your comeback will become another setback if you focus on all the reasons you could fail.

Excuses are comfort zones. Life is never short on excuses.

With only a little bit of effort, we can come up with justifications that ultimately leave us bitter, broken, or numb. Of course, many of us don't see that those justifications have been creeping into us for quite some time. Have you experienced a time when you should be flourishing, but somehow your past experiences with trauma lured you in to settling for the safety of immobility? Maybe you convinced yourself that staying the same meant you'd never hurt again either.

Maybe you convinced yourself that staying the same meant you'd never hurt again either.

We choose to view our future through the lens of past disappointments. That perspective isolates us inside paralyzing fear.

Once our lives have been disturbed by pain, we create a list of personal dos and don'ts out of trepidation. "I'll never trust, try, love, write, believe, hope, sing, laugh, dream, etc., again." Our list of "I'll nevers" is false protection against another letdown. The walls our fears erect are as unstable as the excuses that created them. Placing our hearts in a fortress will not keep pain at a distance. Pain touches every life, but if you're open, it will also teach you a valuable life lesson.

Name Your Pain

If you're going to combat the negative mentality that ultimately sets you up for failure, you must battle excuses with truth. A lifestyle of excuses didn't happen overnight; it was practiced until it became a perfected and comfortable norm. So if we're going to create a new precedent in our lives, we have to understand how our previous pattern was birthed. You cannot change a past you won't confront.

There are two essential truths that will help you realize the potential of restoration. The first is this: you must name your pain. Every pain we've experienced has changed us. No matter how many times you say, "I'm okay," if you haven't accepted and admitted that you've been hurt, you're not healing; you're reverting.

Regardless of what our pride may have us believe, moving on does not mean allowing our lives to go back to the way they were. By definition, *reverting* is going back to a previous state or re-acquiring original features. It's important that you know this: your heart will not return to its original pre-hurt state. *Nor should it.* Doing so would mean that you would have to relinquish the wisdom, growth, and experiences that were designed to make your heart stronger. In haste to move past pain, we often choose the identity most accessible to us, and it's generally a modified/amplified version of who we were before we became acquainted with disappointment. When pain shackles us to difficult memories, we may ignore our wounds and stifle our cries for help. We choose to say we're okay when in actuality, we're just numb.

As you acknowledge your pain and discover how the experience changed you, do not forget the second truth our restoration requires: survival empowers; it does not confine. The mere fact that you're holding this book in your hands is a testament that your spirit is not broken. In spite of your most critical thoughts, something in you knows you have more left than you've lost. The true testimony of survival is not in what you survived; it is in how you were able to truly live again. What good is surviving a break if you still choose to live with a cast? A cast was never meant to be a permanent fixture in your healing.

So you've received the gift of survival. The next step is learning how to use it, which will force you to exercise faith like never before. The moment you begin to reestablish faith in your life, fear will try to rear its ugly head.

Most people struggling to overcome their fears have had an encounter with disappointment so great that every dream they can conceive is contaminated with the toxic anxiety of failure. When your mind becomes cluttered with the possibilities of "what if," there is no room for faith. Living life prepared for the worst possible outcome is like living in a cage—it's not freedom. Over time, you will recognize the difference between guarding your heart and restricting it. You'll learn to stop talking yourself out of the good things God has promised to all who live according to His purpose.

You, my survivor friend, will not settle for a life dictated by insecurities or previous experiences. At this very moment, you are changing the trajectory of your life. You have access to power that is capable of working within you to free you from any mental and emotional bondage that has convinced you a better life is not within your grasp.

Keep the Promises You Make to Yourself

We cannot tap into that power and hang on to excuses at the same time. Your heart, mind, and hands must be free to lay hold of all that is ahead of you. Understanding the psychology of your excuses is pivotal in having permanent victory over them. So, my question to you is:

When did you learn to give up on yourself?

When my daughter began school, she had difficulty differentiating between appropriate times to socialize and moments when focus was mandatory. She's an intelligent and witty little girl, so my husband and I knew we could speak to her practically about the matter. At the conclusion of our conversation, she said, "I'll try my best." My husband's response left me evaluating my own language. He told her that the word *try* leaves room for failure where it isn't necessary. His statement crystalized in my mind, and I realized how often we relieve ourselves of the discipline required to manifest our goals.

Shedding excuses is a discipline that must be practiced with our thoughts, communication, and actions. There is only room for language that declares: *I will!* I'm so glad my daughter is learning this now. We must learn to practice integrity with ourselves before we can reasonably expect to receive it from anyone else.

We must learn to practice integrity with ourselves before we can reasonably expect to receive it from anyone else.

So I'm working on keeping the vows I make to myself. Even small ones like "I will *not* eat dessert when I go out to dinner." After the meal, waiters walk by carrying delicious desserts ordered by other patrons and my resolve weakens. The smells tempt me and I begin internally bargaining. I reason that chocolate comes from a bean, which makes it a vegetable. I recount the nutritional value of vitamin D to justify the ice cream. Before I know it, my spoon is poised and I'm prepared to break the promise I made to my waistline and myself just hours before!

Instant gratification often results in long-term disappointment. The many broken promises I have made to myself have created wounds I am still discovering. Growth occurs when we confront our personal experiences and how they've changed us.

You can create a new pattern and move forward with determination like never before, but you must learn what's stopped you in the past. If the challenge to heal and become whole has been issued by people other than yourself, then your journey will always require permission before progression. Don't allow your destiny to be determined by a democracy. Your immediate circle may not know how to coach you through your heartbreak or, even worse, they may need the company of your misery to distract them from their own need for healing. Avoid the temptation to make your healing contingent on approval and validation from other people. Those who have overcome did so not because it was convenient for other people, but because they simply could not stay in the place where pain met and left them.

Maybe you have made the decision to move forward with your life before. But this time you're not going to try. *You will.* Too much depends on it. As we unravel the lessons of your past, I challenge you to open yourself up fully. Don't allow the fear of facing old decisions and memories make you resist change. You're strong enough to confront your own truth. It may require admitting you've been wrong, or maybe abused, but remember the paradox of the insecure little girl and the confident woman. The bridge from who you once were to who God has ordained you to be is created from bricks of vulnerability, humility as strong as mortar, and a master plan so perfect, even the things that once hurt you will serve in making you better.

Your willingness to let go of the excuses and vow to move forward just laid the first brick, but there's still work to be done. In the next chapter we'll focus on the areas in our lives that we know are present but often choose to ignore. We all know that we aren't perfect, but we've avoided necessary change. Until now! It's time for some intense self-evaluation so that you can recognize the vulnerabilities that exist in your process.

2

Find Your Weeds

When I close my eyes, the questions swarm around my mind like bees in their hive. Why me? When did I change? Can I ever go back to the way things were or was too much damage done? Please, God, if You're still looking over me, help me to retrace the steps that led to my brokenness so that I can discover the lessons You want me to learn from these wounds.

Our beautiful blended family is made up of six children who are each talented, kind, and unique in their own right. Twenty years separate the oldest from the youngest, so we're pretty much in every stage of parenting, all at one time. Not too long after the birth of our daughter Ella, we noticed that we were all trying to adjust to our new identity as a family and really needed some quality family time. My husband and I were tired, our children each needed affirmation about their irreplaceable roles in our lives, homework routines were altered, dinner was a matter of which restaurants could deliver, extracurricular activities were nonexistent, and did I mention my husband and I were tired?

Family Outing

Touré and I knew that we needed to go the extra mile to make sure our family bonded as a unit, so we decided it was time for a family day. There was only one possible day that was free for everyone: Sunday. My husband is a pastor, and having grown up in church, I grew accustomed to Sundays being reserved solely for church services and after-church naps. However, because we were still trying to find our rhythm and balance as a family with a newborn, he made the difficult and necessary decision to have a guest speaker for Sunday. We each loaded our vehicles with children and set out to spend the day enjoying brunch and a movie. Our oldest daughter, Ren, was in the car with me as we listened with agony to our newest family member, Ella, wailing uncontrollably in her car seat.

The moment I pulled into a parking spot and turned off the engine, Ren unbuckled and rushed to rescue her baby sister. It didn't take long before our other four children surrounded Ella, hoping to calm her down from the ride. As we watched our six children walk just a few feet ahead of us toward the restaurant, I grabbed my husband's hand. I was locked in a trance watching our daughter carrying her baby sister in her arms, trying to calm her. Anyone watching might have seen it for what it was—an incredible older sibling holding her baby sister. But for someone who'd experienced teenage pregnancy like me, it might've seemed like the interaction between a young mother and her new baby.

Before I knew it, I was seeing a vivid flashback of me with my baby son, Malachi, when I was just fourteen years old. In an instant I remembered how uncertain I felt about my potential during that time. You could have never told that young girl her journey would become a witness to grace for so many people. No, in that moment all I was trying to do was survive.

It took a few days before I could express to my husband what I experienced that day. As if I were having an out-of-body experience, I told him about the moment that made me flash back to that period in my life. I tried to make the observation sound casual, but the more I verbalized my feelings, tears became inevitable. "It must have been really hard to have a baby at fourteen," Touré said.

Together we talked about the difficulty that I'd silently endured during that time. During my pregnancy, I was surrounded by thousands of people each Sunday. Membership at our church topped more than thirty thousand. I have four siblings and many friends who have become like family, but still, I wrestled with many, many difficult emotions alone. Being raised in an environment with a built-in platform caused me to be even more self-conscious than the average teenager, which is saying something. I began to wonder constantly what other people saw when they looked at me. I became so obsessed with other people's opinions of me that I didn't take time to truly examine my heart. I withdrew on the inside and sought validation through what looked like success on the outside.

I became so obsessed with other people's opinions of me that I didn't take time to truly examine my heart.

I'm learning that surviving painful experiences is good, but the danger comes when we don't take time to actually recover. It's surviving a broken bone and then choosing to live with a perpetual limp rather than undergoing surgery to fix it. Eventually you can learn to function in such a way that won't exacerbate the break, but the rest of your body has to overcompensate to make up for the immobility of that broken bone. Before you know it, you've robbed yourself of the recovery that would restore the full function of your body.

Guard Your Heart

This is what happens to all of us when we don't take time to find and pull the weeds that are created after we've experienced difficulty in life. One of my favorite scriptures in Proverbs speaks directly to this issue: "Guard your heart above all else, for it determines the course of your life" (4:23 NLT). Of the many lessons we learn from life and in school, the one that often gets the least amount of discussion is learning to guard your heart. We learn mathematical equations, linguistic skills, vocabulary, and science, but how much more valuable is the skill of keeping negative thoughts and experiences from taking root in the heart?

As I've meditated on the need to guard the heart, I've begun to think of my heart as a garden worth cultivating and protecting. The Bible shows us so many examples of gardens created for both beauty and sustenance. We also see that such beauty attracts predators. In the garden of Eden that predator came in the form of a serpent. Remember how God told Adam and Eve to be fruitful and multiply? By providing the garden of Eden, He gave them an example in which to model their fruit so that they would understand what was worth multiplying on the earth.

We all know that Eve's desire to know and see more than what God provided ultimately allowed the serpent to distract her from her purpose. Eve's sin was not that the serpent got into the garden. Her sin was that she allowed the serpent to have access to her mind. Guarding your heart does not mean that bad things won't happen to you. It means that you won't allow those bad things to take root and produce fruit in your mind. Weeds of fear and insecurity leave only room for internal negativity and hopelessness.

If we want to guard the garden of the heart, we have many options to keep potential pests at bay, but there isn't an enemy to gardens more constant and nagging than weeds. Weeds spring up in gardens where healthy plants have not been cultivated. The same is true in our lives. There are times when we've been wounded and, whether through preoccupation or neglect, we've ignored certain areas. Then issues spring up and we wonder why.

At this point in your journey, your heart is probably a garden full of both fruit and weeds that your thoughts, emotions, and experiences have produced. It feels good to see all that beauty and fruit, but I challenge you to look for the weeds. And be willing to pull them out by the roots or risk spoiling the beauty and fruitfulness of your heart.

There are weeds in your life you are aware of and others that you are still discovering. Those weeds could be blocking you from having meaningful connections and liberty in your life. After you identify and pull out the weeds, you have to implement a plan of defense against them. You must filter your thoughts and actions with the knowledge that those weeds produced an unhealthy pattern in your life.

The Weed of Defensiveness

The weeds were thick in my life when I set out on my mission to survive after my teen pregnancy. I told myself I could not afford to make any more mistakes. Of course, I made *plenty* of mistakes after my pregnancy, but instead of owning them, I ignored anyone whose presence would serve as a reminder of the higher expectations I once held for myself. I was slowly but surely disconnecting from family and friends as my life was choked by the weeds.

Turns out I can't stand being wrong. It's one of my least favorite feelings. I hate it so much I'm embarrassed to admit that I've become stubborn about it. If you would have asked me five years ago if I had a problem admitting when I'm wrong, I would have said no or it doesn't happen frequently enough for it to be an issue in my life. The truth is that it happened frequently, but I was so blinded by pride that I couldn't answer truthfully. It wasn't until I met my husband that I began weighing the possibility that I don't do everything perfectly. This is where you can insert my dramatic facial expression of pure shock.

But God brought me a partner in life who is much more than a cuddle buddy. He's a God-given mate so intimately connected to me that he's able to point out the inclinations and patterns that could be detrimental to our relationship and my personal growth. That's the way God designed it to be.

When we met it had been more than a year since I'd left an unhealthy relationship. My heart had finally come to a place where I felt genuine inner peace and confidence. Then along came Touré—a man every bit worthy of the title "Prince Charming." We began to go beyond the surface talks of courting and really began to lay the foundation that has sustained our relationship. I can remember how completely vulnerable and naked I felt the first time he pointed out an area I needed to work on. My first reaction was to deflect and respond with a list of his qualities that could use some improvement. On the inside my pride was screaming, *Please don't tell me I'm not perfect!* I knew I wasn't perfect by the sheer fact that I'm human. Still, I didn't like it.

God regularly uses the safety of my relationship with Touré to knock me off of my high horse and force me to take a deeper look into my heart. When Touré noticed that I am often very slow to admit when I'm wrong, I took some time to process his observation. Perhaps, I rationalized, it's not that I have a problem admitting I'm wrong; it's just that I need to first justify why I have the right to be wrong. In other words, I was defensive. Our disagreements would generally begin with me taking time to explain the path that led to my error rather than admitting one had happened in the first place.

After a few more times of him bringing up this behavior, I decided to really trace the source of this weed in my life. Turns out my pattern of not admitting that I was wrong was rooted in a fear I've held since becoming a teenage mother. One of my greatest fears was that my life would be judged by the decisions that led to me becoming a teenage mother. In response, I resolved to distance myself from that time in my life. This overcompensation ultimately led to me placing more value on being right than on learning from being wrong. I thought that I could balance misconceptions about me with a narrative of a girl who had turned her life around and had never made any other mistakes. I wanted to convince people I'd achieved perfection after imperfection. But how ridiculous is that when life is full of experiences that can teach us lessons through our mistakes?

Fast-forward years down the road and the result of my insecurity was a woman who has a hard time apologizing to people affected by my choices. That's just one of the many things I've discovered from tracing my action to the emotion in my heart that produced it.

How About You?

What are your weeds? What thoughts and behaviors are keeping you from enjoying the full beauty of the heart God has given you? Your willingness to seek them out will transform your heart, producing compassion and creating opportunities to extend grace to others. The only way to remove the weeds is to combat them with humility. The fruit of such examination is not constant shame; it's simple humility and grace.

What keeps us from taking a moment to pause and reflect on the steps we've taken in life? For me, this "weeding" meant facing some ugly truths. That I wasn't the confident adolescent I pretended to be. That I felt lost. That I was in a situation bigger than I could handle on my own. So instead I sought external validation. Of course others' opinions can never offer true inner confidence and self-acceptance. Yet like a drug that provides a temporary high, validation from others offers a distraction from the insecurities that scream within us. The desire to relentlessly seek praise from other people is a sign that there is an emptiness within us that can only be discovered by honest self-examination. Sometimes we can't even fully comprehend what our lack is because we're too busy pretending we don't have any.

Making Good Decisions

Everything from your style of communication to your moral compass has been shaped by life experiences. Those experiences, positive or negative, have made you who you are today. Until you begin to question why you think and feel the way you do, you'll never be able to have a thriving life. You can't afford to allow actions that are rooted in fear or insecurities to continue to flourish in your life. Fear-based decision-making will only produce more fear. It's important to recognize that the external successes in life are not necessarily a reflection of a healthy soul. In fact, many people are able to capitalize on their insecurities by creating outlets that attract popularity and wealth.

While some people amass riches and attention, their insides are often haunted by fear. This is why it's important not to compare your life to what appears to be working for other people. True success cannot be seen with the human eye, but it can be felt through genuine warmth and connection. We live in a culture that often celebrates outward achievements with little regard for internal prosperity. I am reminded of Jesus' words: "For what does it profit a man to gain the whole world and forfeit his soul?" (Mark 8:36 ESV).

Many of the indicators we use to determine triumph over difficulty are tangible, but our greatest accomplishment comes when we have the ability to master our souls. Having an awareness of your issues and guarding your life against them is pivotal in the pursuit of soul mastery. If you're like me and you struggle to admit when you're wrong, you'll have to find the humility to apologize before you even think about justifying what happened. You'll have to examine arguments from other people's perspectives. You may have to begin saying things like, "I apologize that we've disconnected on this. It's important to me that we're able to get on the same page. Please tell me how my actions affected you."

With an open heart and mind, we must be willing to accept that some situations aren't about right or wrong; they're about peace. If only life was as cut and dried as right and wrong. When it comes to connecting with other people, remember that while your actions may seem right in your eyes, they may be wrong in the eyes of someone else, and most important, in God's eyes. In other words, despite your best intentions, sometimes the people in your life will be hurt by your actions. There will be times when you make decisions and your eyes aren't opened until after damage has been done. This does not make you a bad person; it means that you're human. But if you're constantly walking away every time you hurt someone, you'll never experience the power of love that restores trust and fosters forgiveness. Their hurt doesn't mean you should walk away. Actually, it's an opportunity for you to own your mistake and offer them the restoration you never received.

Contrary to popular belief we do not just stumble into our decisions. Every emotion is connected to a thought and those thoughts produce action. Consciously or subconsciously, we've actively played a role in perpetuating whatever disdain we've come to associate with certain areas of our lives. And if we don't think of our past, present, or future with compassion and care, we'll ultimately resent the parts of our hearts that need love the most.

Consciously or subconsciously, we've actively played a role in perpetuating whatever disdain we've come to associate with certain areas of our lives.

Before delving into the layers that have created your sense of identity, there are a few factors that are imperative for you to remember. The first is that from the moment you were conceived in your mother's womb, God called your life beautiful. He knows and sees everything about your life. He sees the decisions you have yet to make and the ones that have left you hurting. If you're still struggling to accept that truth, I understand why. It may sound cliché and overly used, especially to people who've grown up in church, but it's only because it's the most powerful concept one can ever fully master.

As you read this book, there may be times when you feel the weight of facing your truth is too great. There may be times when you question whether or not you have the courage to open the doors of your heart that you've been comfortable keeping closed.

Remember this: you are strong enough to confront your history. Don't turn away from your brokenness. Remember that you're not doing this alone. God foreknew this moment would come. Every now and then we need a reminder that someone else has defeated a giant we must face. Allow this book to be that reminder. Instead of counting the reasons you have to be afraid, give yourself permission to be brave. You've already survived the trauma, but you can't transform your pain into purpose until you're willing to pick it up again. Roll up your sleeves, wipe your tears, and boldly embrace your truth.

You cannot begin to guard your heart until you fully know your heart. Beware of looking solely at the noteworthy accolades you have received, for that is a recipe for pride, not true confidence. Instead take a journey from your childhood to present day and see all you have become. Recognize there have been moments where you felt like giving up, but you found the strength to keep moving. Think about the times you knew you should have walked away but convinced yourself to stay. How did you get to that place? Remember this isn't an invitation for shame. It's a plea from your heart to look honestly at what has shaped it. It's an opportunity to pull the weeds from the garden of your heart. Pulling those weeds will make the garden of your heart fruitful and beautiful.

3

Learn Your Patterns

She was so afraid . . . that girl I used to be. She thought that she was just one opinion, one lie, one truth away from having the most vulnerable parts of her life exposed. Her fear convinced her to hide away the essence of her soul and even the prayers that would make her whole. She caved into the pressure to be like everyone else and robbed the world of the wealth assigned to her truth. She was a lonely girl, that girl I used to be, but one would never know it because she wore a disguise so popular that it eventually became her worst enemy. Her disguise was the lie she told herself and the truth she was unwilling to face.

"What Had Happened Was . . ."

For as long as I can remember, whenever someone in my family prefaced a story with "what had happened was . . ." we knew we were in for a long, dramatic, and hilarious story. Those four words might make grammar teachers cringe, but for us they signaled a trip down memory lane. We anxiously sat on the edge of our seats waiting to hear all the narrator's fabulous details. In moments like those, facing the past wasn't scary.

Those stories often left us laughing until we cried. But when life deprives us of laughter and leaves only the taste of salty tears and painful memories, those four words, *what had happened was*, are slow to surface.

When teen pregnancy was no longer a stranger's issue but my reality, I didn't think back to "what had happened was." I became so consumed with distancing myself from my mistake that I failed to learn from it. Hindsight is only 20/20 for those who take a moment to look behind them.

I spent many years trying to maintain a persona, which is problematic because I could not discover my authentic identity as long as I was pretending. There's nothing wrong with not having figured out who you are, but so much can go wrong when you pretend that you have. There is a recurring theme that I have discovered when listening to the stories of people from around the world. We want so badly to convince ourselves that we have it all together that we miss the opportunity to truly come to a place of inner peace. It's okay that you don't have all of the answers regarding your life. Faking joy in the face of misery or peace when you have inner turmoil is dangerous.

Had I looked back in the months after my teen pregnancy, I would have learned that I cared too much about the opinions of my peers. While this may seem like normal teenage behavior, what made my mentality unhealthy was the lengths to which I was willing to go in order to satisfy others' expectations of me. This observation may not have prevented my teen pregnancy, but it would have helped me avoid subsequent painful life decisions I made from that point on. The same need for acceptance and validation would haunt me when I emerged in different social set-tings. I could have become more self-aware of my tendency to gain attention and acceptance by any means necessary. That revelation would have allowed me to place limitations on how and to what lengths I was willing to indulge in certain relationships.

Oftentimes our disposition for not looking back is rooted in the fact that we can't change what happened. Maybe you have set boundaries for the people you've allowed into your life but haven't set boundaries for yourself. Such necessary boundaries develop character and integrity. You must be willing to ask yourself if you're making a decision from a place of fear and insecurity or from the strength necessary to maintain your esteem. Fear-based decisions yield devastating results. If you've chosen to maintain an unhealthy mind-set out of fear of starting over, you will never be able to realize the full potential of your life.

Now, let's take a moment to dissect your pattern. Are you surrounded by people who constantly take from you but add very little to your life? Ever wonder why these types of people are attracted to you? Better yet, have you ever wondered why you con-tinue to attract those types of people? Many people feel a sense of value when they are needed by other people, even if that parti-

Fear-based decisions yield devastating results.

cular need turns into codependency. It may be because you once felt indispensable and now only feel comfortable in relationships where someone cannot survive without you.

Perhaps you have a difficult time being vulnerable in relation-ships. You may have a history of choosing friends and partners who are emotionally unavailable to you. Their emotional unavail-ability makes you feel rejected, yet you can't seem to walk away.

Oftentimes this is an indication that the connection you long to have with them needs to start with rebuilding the connection you have with yourself.

Or perhaps you have a difficult time receiving love. It could be because abandonment issues have made you believe that people are unreliable and will ultimately walk away. Did your toxic relationship with a parent affect you more than you'd like to admit? Do you have a history of giving yourself to people who fail to see your value? Are you struggling with forgiveness? There could be countless scenarios and situations that have created your pattern, but you must be willing to search for the patterns that have developed in your life that reflect the current state of your soul.

As you dig beneath the surface, you'll begin to understand how your current patterns are truly just manifestations of past emotions.

There will come a time in all of our lives when we face issues that make us feel incomplete. How we process those feelings of inadequacy and learn to form a proper defense against them is critical in moving forward. The facade of recovery where hurt still exists creates an infection that viciously spreads from our hearts and through our actions. Eventually it becomes the standard for what we deem acceptable in our lives.

In order to avoid repeating toxic patterns, we must be diligent in understanding the circumstances that produced them in the first place. Many of us long for intimacy and acceptance from other people, but we fail to master the type of self-discovery that allows us to achieve intimacy within. How can we ask someone to love our hearts if we don't even know?

There are many variables that make the thought of unraveling our decisions and retracing our steps frightening. If we're going to commit to achieving a positive outlook on things that once devastated us, we will have to believe that the worst things that happened to us have the potential to work for our benefit. Many of us unwittingly give our power away by living in a version of our stories that only leaves room for us to be a victim. There are moments in life when we find ourselves victimized, but such a moment does not have to become our identity.

No Longer a Victim

The word *victim* derives from the fifteenth-century Latin word *victima*. In its original context the word was used to denote a creature killed as a religious sacrifice. The meaning of that word has since evolved to its current definition, "a person who is hurt, tortured, or killed by another." While both definitions hold similarities, there is an important word in the fifteenth-century derivative that has not passed the test of time: *sacrifice*. At some point between the fifteenth century and the eighteenth century the definition began to focus more on the pain that exists and not the sense of loss that leaves many feeling as though they've been sacrificed.

The poison that taints our memories of the past didn't just come from the hurt we experienced; it also came from the sacrifices we made to endure those moments. While we strive to take a look back at our history, we may mourn the things we feel we lost. That loss may have been even more extreme than the pain of the hurt.

Some of you had an outside perpetrator who victimized you. Others had unhealthy, internal thought patterns that you allowed to have too much control over your actions. Still others of you may have become so comfortable in your decisions that you chose to turn a blind eye to that destructive behavior. Though the crimes may vary, the shame that comes with feeling as though we've been robbed is universal. That feeling of loss halts us from ever reliving those moments again. But, I've got good news for you. The moments that left you feeling shattered are the most instrumental in producing your healing. That may be a thought too unfathomable to conceive, but it creates a beautiful and necessary vulnerability.

It can become so easy to set boundaries for the people we allow to come into our lives, but very rarely do we take a moment to create boundaries for ourselves. These necessary boundaries develop character and integrity after our downfalls.

Maybe you rationalize that looking back is pointless because the past is past and we can't change what happened. Though this is true, we can avoid subsequent mistakes and patterns through self-introspection.

Hindsight Is 20/20

You know how people say that hindsight is 20/20? I did not always understand that. Like many people I tried to avoid looking back as much as possible. I wish I could tell you that it was for some noble reason like I was so optimistic about my future that my past didn't matter. No, my unwillingness to look back was rooted in the fear that I would not like or understand what I saw about myself. I did not want to face the memories that made me feel shame. The problem with avoiding the lessons of our past is that we're bound to repeat them in the future. An unexamined past will always threaten to contaminate the potential of our present.

Fortunately, I've learned that looking back does not have to be painful. When looking back over my past, I had to learn to do so with compassion, understanding, and love. I was often my harshest critic when recounting the twists and turns of my life experiences. Once I came to a place of self-acceptance and awareness of God's love, I was able to look back over my life with sensitivity.

It's important that you learn to handle your heart with care. Regardless of how tough or strong you feel you are, there are delicate parts on the inside of us. If we do not learn to respect our vulnerability, we cannot teach others to do the same. Of course I haven't always had that revelation. I could not become aware of the power my past possessed because I was constantly running away from it. I hoped that I could distance myself from my choices and decisions in such a way that they would no longer be a part of the fabric of who I am. If you are like me and have made choices that you haven't always been proud of, you may have been tempted to do the same. I hope it encourages you to know that you aren't alone.

I also hope to challenge you in this chapter to discover the silent, toxic patterns that produced outcomes in your life that make you shudder. Behind the shivers of shame and regret that often make us run and hide from our history are the keys that unlock futures more beautiful than we can fathom.

I have a history of living my life too concerned with how other people viewed me. I cared so much about what people thought of me that I never took time to assess my own thoughts. If I experienced something with someone, I did not consider how that experience affected me, only how/if it would alter what that person thought of me. My pattern of seeking acceptance and validation was rooted in fear of rejection. My fear of rejection was a result of feeling inadequate. A mind-set of inadequacy convinced me that the only way I would receive validation was to create an illusion of perfection and confidence. The manufacturing of this illusion began long before adulthood. It first surfaced when I was a preteen entering into adolescence.

Moments That Trigger Shame, Pain, Embarrassment

The problem with illusions is that they're constantly confronted by reality. When those moments occur one must choose between standing on their truth or finding another space for their facade to live. I became disloyal to my truth in hopes of receiving acceptance from my peers when I was a teenager. I would lie or conveniently withhold the truth about my teen pregnancy. I did not want my son's existence to complicate friendships or relationships. In school environments where people were not privy to the full scope of my life, I was just a "normal" teenager.

However, as I mentioned, illusions are always confronted by reality. That moment came for me when I was in the lunchroom of my high school with my older sister Cora. A heated debate about teen pregnancy ensued and my sister became argumentative. The subject matter obviously hit very close to home and my sister did not appreciate the negative remarks that were being made about teen mothers. I sat in the corner of the room praying that God would perform a miracle and I would discreetly evaporate. My prayer was interrupted by my sister blurting out something to the effect of, "Well, my sister's a teenage mother and she's not a hoe!" There it was. My truth laid bare for all of my classmates to see. I was mortified. As embarrassing as the moment was, I look back now and realize that no one really cared.

The memory sticks out in my mind as if it just happened yesterday. However, outside of an initial awkward silence, I don't remember anyone treating me differently or shunning me. Perhaps I was more concerned about my truth than any of them were. That reality should have changed my ability to engage with the world, but it did not. I still continued to live life more concerned with how people would handle my truth than taking time to fully embrace it myself. This was a pattern that followed me through adulthood.

What Are Your Patterns?

Have you ever taken time to consider your own emotional patterns? As we talked about thoughts producing emotions and emotions producing actions, we must go one step further and consider the repeated thoughts that create recurring emotions and therefore yield habitual actions. Understanding those patterns will require opening the dark closets of our hearts and dissecting the memories we thought were buried. We must begin to ask ourselves: Why did this happen to me? What did it teach me? How do I keep it from ever happening again?

I doubt there is a more insecure time in a person's life than the teen years. Pimples begin forming, bodies begin changing, voices begin to crack, emotions explode, and communication is non-existent. Being a teenager is culture shock! It's one of the first times we're unsupervised in the outside world. This exposure allows for connection with other people. Adolescence was probably one of the first times you realized just how many variables it takes to produce a successful life. Adolescence reveals the unprecedented discipline, social stresses, expectations, and familial changes that are an unavoidable part of life.

You probably had your first encounter with the unlimited dilemmas of life during your adolescent years. It is during this time that each of us begins to recognize how painful and disappointing life can be. If you're fortunate enough to have experienced a childhood that was free from trauma, then adolescence is when you begin to realize that your history may be an anomaly for some people. We often believe everyone was raised in a similar environment to our own. As our worlds begin to cross-pollinate, the exploration of other people's history becomes intriguing. When you're a teenager, you realize that the mysterious world of being a grown-up is more complicated than it seems. No longer can adults talk over your head; we often learn hard truths that jade our perspective. Suddenly experiences like divorce, job loss, abandonment, and rejection are no longer temporary ailments that can be cured with lollipops and kisses.

We begin to want explanations about, or shelter from, the issues that plague us. Our naiveté and pain can give us harsh views of the world that scar our adulthood. The problem with our teenage years is that often our observations are valid, but our perspective is very limited. It's not until we're older that we begin to tap into the compassion necessary to learn from those observations.

As a parent, I'm beginning to see more clearly just how challenging adolescence is. Though you have some idea of who you are, you're unsure of how you compare in the world. The need for acceptance often creates personas that we manifest from insecurities. Those personas follow us through adolescence and into adulthood until we're no longer sure who we are at our core.

Of course, when I was a teenager, I did not realize just how little I knew about life. I felt pressure to define myself. I was ambitious. My parents may have considered it rebellious, but they're not writing the book so we'll just go with my side of the story. Ambition is great, but ambition without wisdom is like a car with no brakes. You may get where you're going, but you'll cause a lot of damage along the way. My ambition led me to break many of the rules that existed in my household. I wanted what I wanted so badly that I didn't care what it took to get it.

It wasn't until I was filing for divorce after four years of marriage that I realized that my ambition was raw material that needed to be studied, shaped, formed, and directed with intentionality. Later on, that ambition allowed for many wonderful opportunities in my life, but it was not until I recognized the blessing and the curse of it that I was able to fully use it for good.

The patterns in your life will determine the difference between the destruction of your life or the construction of it. It's up to you to choose.

Unfortunately comparison does not leave much room for appreciation of the positive things that may exist in the world. That's because teen years almost always center on our deficiency. At the core of our wondering are the questions: Am I enough? Did I receive enough? Can I compete when I don't feel like I measure up? Often frustrated adults fail to remember what it was like when they were in those formative years and fail to convey that that level of self-inquiry exists long after your age no longer has "teen" at the end of it. The earlier we're able to identify our insecurities, the better we'll be at guarding our decisions against them. The last thing you want is to create a life that has been built on fear.

Teenagers quest in hopes that they will discover what they wished they had received. That search for fulfillment often leads to even more disappointment. The holes in your life were not meant to be filled with substitutes for real love or the affirmation of attention. The holes in your life that have made you feel the most empty were created to be filled with the knowledge of God. You may not always recognize the knowledge of God when you're in the midst of sorting through the messes of life, but His sovereignty is all about taking issues that once seemed hopeless and producing life anew. Accepting the knowledge of God is not just believing that He is real, but trusting that even your darkest moments were created so that light could shine through you.

> *The holes in your life that have made you feel the most empty were created to be filled with the knowledge of God.*

Good Patterns

Of course not all patterns are bad. Some patterns are so virtuous that they should be refined and held for a lifetime. The greatest gift you can give yourself is the ability to identify patterns that have created themes in your life. Those patterns may not go away completely, but it's possible that you can begin to recognize them and diminish the power they have to control your life. I've had to work extra hard at pinpointing my emotions and expressing them when necessary. When you notice a shift in your mood, take a moment to truly take inventory of what led to the shift. Don't just chock it up to being off-center. Find the root of what's blocking you from having complete joy. You would be surprised how much simply expressing those emotions can relieve you.

Prayer's Power

For me, that's the power of prayer. It's not about fancy words or auspicious speech. Prayer is about the peace you receive when you invite God into what concerns you. Sure, He already knows everything, but His power is not unleashed until you're able to express to Him where you are. Not sharing your troubles with God is like driving in a car with navigation, but not inputting the address to your destination. If you haven't tapped in to the system that is available to you, you spend more time lost than necessary. Open up to Him and admit that you've discovered some parts of you that have been lost or confused in the process.

God will grant you the wisdom and discernment to see the patterns that prohibit you from experiencing true satisfaction in Him. You don't have to be limited because of what you haven't seen. For instance, just because you were raised in a home where abuse was prevalent doesn't mean you can't have fulfilling relationships. You can create a new culture for your family. You can do anything you put your mind to if you are willing to transform your mind by releasing the paradigms that trapped you.

Mercy in Reflection

Mercy Ministries, headquartered in Nashville, Tennessee, is dedicated to helping young women confront traumas that have the potential to oppress and depress them. I had the privilege of visiting this amazing place. It's a safe place for victims of unfortunate life circumstances, often teenagers, to come and be enveloped by the love of God. During their stay they're able to meet with other girls who have had similar struggles. With the help of counselors, special guest speakers, and a team of support staff, the young women are encouraged to examine their lives without judgment or shame.

I could not help but wish I had been able to stay at a place like Mercy when I was pregnant with my son. Much of what these young women are able to accomplish in the months that they are there it took me many years to learn. Before that thought could even begin to form regret in my mind, it was replaced by the peace of knowing that it doesn't matter how long it took me to have peace about my past; what matters is that I arrived.

Regardless of how much time has passed since your trauma, it's never too late to look back on your life and learn. To be reminded that God has created rest stops along your journey that offer you the same level of safety and breakthrough available to the girls at Mercy. The truth is that it doesn't matter whether you're in a shelter, a mansion in Beverly Hills, or a home in Minnesota; you will not magically come to a place of peace in your life. It takes great courage, intentionality, and work to confront unhealthy patterns.

Before moving on to the next chapter, I want to challenge you to take a moment and reflect. Can you remember areas in your life where you felt shame, pain, or embarrassment? Are there specific memories attached to that? How did your perspective on yourself and others change as a result of that? Recognizing the root of your pattern is the only way you can eradicate it from your life.

Once you begin to realize some of the unhealthy patterns associated with your life, you have to wage a defense against them. That defense will have to come in the form of combatting those thoughts or emotions with a prevailing healthier thought. For instance, instead of saying, "God can't use someone like me after all that I've done," you have to pray, "God, my breath is a sign that You need me on this earth. Show me how my life can make this world a better place. I'm willing to sacrifice my pride, ego, and plans for Yours." Vulnerability with God releases the power that negativity has over your life. There are some issues in our lives too great for us to handle on our own. We need divine interventions to remind us that there is a resource available to us that supercedes the obstacles around us. You're not fighting this battle on your own. God has a perfect plan and will for your life. Trust His plan, which includes joy, peace, and love. That's the transformational thinking that provides a light in even the darkest tunnels. As we journey through that tunnel, we will take a look not only at your role but also at how the role of family and friends has defined your ability to function in the world.

4

Know Your Roots

I know I should be, but I'm not always proud of where I came from. Don't get me wrong, there's beauty woven in the tapestry of my DNA, but there's a lot of pain as well. Pain we haven't addressed, issues we don't discuss, and questions lay silent. I don't know how to break the cycle that has created comfort and dysfunction for generations. God, give me the strength to be an example in my family that we have the power to use our pain for purpose.

My paternal grandmother, Odith, was a gun-toting, sanctified-cussing firecracker from West Virginia. She was a no-nonsense woman who placed high value on education and entrepreneurism. My maternal grandmother was a macaroni and cheese–cooking, button-sewing, sanctified-cussing hospitality queen from West Virginia. She specialized in making sure we had loads of Vaseline on our knees and elbows and presents under the tree when my parents couldn't afford Christmas. I've got fire and power running through my veins. My father writes like a spiritual poet, my mother can tell you to go to hell with such class and grace that you look forward to the trip.

You mix all that together, and you have me. I consider myself to be mostly sane with a few buttons you should never push. There are moments when my mother's words come out of my mouth and it scares me. There have been times when I have read something I wrote and had to question if I was merely reciting verbatim something my father had written or if it were my original thought. The reason I've heard my mother's words escape my lips and seen my father's writing staring back at me is because regardless of how unique my existence is, I have been shaped by the environment I was raised in.

Pre-Existing Conditions

Have you ever been to a new doctor for the first time and been handed the dreaded clipboard? Mountains of paperwork ask everything from your name to how long your pinky toe is. Then there's the part that often has us breaking out our phones to text our parents or scratching our heads in guessing. The sheets that have the most questions ask you to detail your family history, everything from allergies, cancer, diabetes, high blood pressure, cholesterol, nose bleeds, and so on and so on. It feels like the list has every possible malady humankind has ever experienced. Doctors know that if your family wrestled with certain medical conditions, you're susceptible to them too.

Patients who have discussed such things with their families come in armed and equipped with the knowledge of what to help their doctor look for. Then there are other patients who haven't had that level of communication in their families and have to mark the box that indicates such unawareness: "unknown." When the doctor reads that answer on the form, he recognizes that his job will require an increased level of attention. He'll have to search for any- and everything that could pose a health risk to his patient.

Much like predisposed genetic conditions, there are other hereditary soul issues we must discover, cure, and guard against within our lives. We've talked about the environments that have shaped us, but what about the unspoken mind-sets that have limited our ability to function healthily? These issues are less talked about than health conditions. They're the mind-sets that set the tone for our interpersonal interactions. As our adult relationships grow and deepen, traces of those emotional heart conditions are evident in all of them. It's not until we're confronted with someone who has been raised differently than we were and we realize that perhaps our families had a way of doing things that differs so drastically from the way someone else was raised that we begin to wonder if it was healthy in the first place.

As I began to connect with other people, I remember struggling to answer questions as simple as, "How do you feel?" I knew how I felt, of course, but I couldn't always find the will to admit those feelings. Relationship after relationship challenged me to find my voice, but there was something standing in the way. I realize now that I'd inherited an emotional pattern. Writing became my outlet and the only way I could truly express myself.

Have you ever taken time to examine the patterns that exist in your life because of the culture you grew up in? Our environments shape us, but what we observe fills us and creates the pattern in which we begin to understand life and people. If we're truly going to maximize our vulnerabilities, we must do so with a goal of maintaining some patterns, but creating new ones where there is a need. A new pattern must be created so that our children's children can be protected from the thoughts that keep us from achieving the best version of ourselves.

Your childhood was a training ground that taught you a combination of what to do and what not to do. What are the unspoken codes and patterns in your life that other people may not fully be able to understand?

Where We've Been

"Secrets, secrets are no fun. Secrets are for everyone." I heard this rhyme often when growing up. When a student was caught whispering to another child, the teacher would interrupt by singing that rhyme. She'd force us to stand up and share with the classroom what was so important that it distracted us from the lesson. The truth of this rhyme came to light as I grew up in church.

Church is one of the dominant experiences that shaped me. Almost everything I've learned about people and the struggles of life derives from what I felt, heard, and experienced in the pews. One of the many things I learned is that everyone has "something." A job, marriage, or kids that can be perceived as normal usually cover that something up, but underneath it all, their something is a secret.

I was often flabbergasted at the hypocrisy of the very people I was sitting beside each Sunday. How could they condemn the lifestyles of people they disagreed with while secretly slipping into an alternate reality that contradicted their public image? I began to believe every person on the planet had a secret they were hiding from the people who presumed they knew them best.

That same circle taught me loyalty. I learned the power of sticking together in hard times. I understood the necessity of doing whatever it takes to get a job done. Tenacity has been pumped in me since before I can remember. I never saw my parents quit when things got tough. I saw obstacle after obstacle make them stronger and wiser.

When History Inhibits Joy

The character trait I found myself having the least amount of hope in was integrity. Blame it on my first marriage failing to infidelity or all of the contradictions I've seen since childhood, but the first time my husband Touré promised me he wouldn't cheat on me, he was met with silence. In my head I was thinking that I'd rather he not make that kind of promise to me. I was in love with everything about him, but life had done a thorough job of convincing me that anything could happen. If I kept the possibilities open, then I'd be less likely to be hurt if/when it did. Or so I thought.

It only took a few more times of Touré making this promise before he eventually asked me why I seemed so uncomfortable each time he pledged his fidelity to me. When I expressed my hesitation to him, I had to be willing to confront the pattern that convinced me trust had limitations. Through a process of discussions and self-examination it became clear that my heart wanted to believe one thing, but the patterns of my environment made me settle for another.

As much as I desired to have a fully committed man, the insecurities of my patterns kept me from fully embracing him. If

I'd already adjusted to the notion of my spouse disappointing me, how could I ever appreciate him treasuring me? I had come to a place where I was willing to live in the moment without fear or concern of what would happen next. Expecting pain in the future takes away your joy in the present. Worrying steals joy that is already yours.

Maybe you have a pattern like the one I had: you know there's something to work on when you should be able to receive love and devotion, but instead fear makes you question whether or not it's real.

If we don't confront our patterns, they will multiply in our families. Our people will learn to live in less than their potential because no one was willing to say "enough is enough." I don't know what your pattern is or who introduced you to it. I'm willing to bet

> *If we don't confront our patterns, they will multiply in our families.*

that there is a mind-set you've adjusted to that permeates throughout your entire family. Whether it's harsh criticism or unwillingness to voice truth, you must be willing to find and slay the giant that stands in the way of inner growth for you and your family.

I can always tell when a little girl has been raised by a bitter woman. Her compliments are laced with disdain and her humor is dry with sarcasm and bitterness. The language of self-hate begins to spew over and sabotages relationships that were meant to be valued, but the negative patterns that form our communication and perspective could not be overcome.

The worst thing you can do is acquiesce and decide that some things will never change so there's no point in trying to confront them. A few negative patterns do not equate to an entire negative upbringing. All of our childhoods are a mixture of good, bad, and ugly things. Our ability to confront the challenging things while still revering the righteous is important.

Determining what you received the most training in is pivotal to becoming self-aware. I recently met a young man whose father placed a significant amount of pressure on him to succeed. His fear of failure was so great that he abandoned any opportunity that required more than he thought he could give. The moment he received correction to help him better handle certain situations, he saw it as rejection. The sense of rejection magnified his insecurity about failure and made him run when he could have grown. Though his father meant well by wanting to establish a healthy sense of drive for his son, he never noticed how the weight of his expectations made his son cave in high-pressure situations.

This is why you must take the time to learn your roots.

The young man did not realize that he was more inclined to run from high-pressure situations because of experiences he had as a child. With just a little bit more knowledge he could have trained himself to stop running when his insecurities told him to take off. Taking the step to dig even further would have revealed to him that his father's fears of him not being successful were rooted in the extreme poverty his father experienced as a child.

Insecurities Create Patterns That Affect Our Relationships

When insecurities lay silently buried within us, they become barriers in our families. Those barriers prohibit our families from fully bridging together to overcome generational mind-sets that limit growth. The sad reality is that your awakening may come before your family is ready to embrace the vulnerability necessary to evolve.

Your freedom cannot be contingent on whether or not you're able to convince others to embark on the journey with you. It's up to you to follow the path that leads to your liberation. Freedom and peace can inspire change within your family. Always remember that you can't force someone to change. God doesn't even do that. Open dialogue can be beneficial in resolving some issues, but both parties must be in a headspace that allows for honest and loving communication.

If the young man I mentioned had chosen to dissect his family's history, it would have allowed him to be more compassionate and forgiving when his father placed that pressure on his shoulders. No one in his family talked about the pressure of having to constantly perform well. It was always brushed off with sayings like, "That's just how he is!" What happens when the normal patterns of your family create difficulty for you when you grow up? Just because things have always been a certain way doesn't mean that they have to stay that way.

You have the power to break the patterns that create confusion in your family. You don't have to spend a lifetime regretting where you came from or what you feel you didn't receive. Avoid the temptation to handicap yourself because you feel as though you've come from an environment that did not prepare you for success.

God is the ultimate Creator. Combining your work and faith with His plan for your life creates momentum that transforms everything that should have stopped you into fuel that propels you into a destiny far greater than you could have imagined. When you come to the realization that you're an agent of change, you won't be deterred by the pre-existing conditions of your family.

You must acknowledge those conditions to set a new tone for your family going forward. You can be the change they've needed to see. The worst thing you can do is attempt to live a life without voicing the hurt you experienced. Open up and confess to God the fears that haunt you. He's seen the tears you've learned to hide. But it's not enough for Him to see them. He needs you to invite Him into those areas by finally becoming vulnerable enough to say "ouch."

For people who have difficulty expressing themselves, the mere notion of admitting that something got under their skin is devastating, but this book is about embracing the uncomfortable. If you allow regret to seep under your skin, but fail to acknowledge and treat it, an infection will run rampant inside of your soul. Seek out the healing balm that is God's grace.

Privacy Versus Secrecy

"What happens in this house stays in this house." These words have been echoed in households like mine all over the country for decades. The terminology is hardly ever evoked in celebratory times. It's when conflict arises that we want to guard our family business. While privacy is helpful, this mandate suggests that what is more critical than the issue at hand is making sure the issue doesn't become public knowledge, or worse, gossip. I have admittedly echoed a similar sentiment while raising my children.

The goal may be privacy, but often the results are alienation, secrecy, and internalization.

Family patterns may adversely affect our ability to relate to others. Some of those patterns can be as simple as we don't express our feelings to being brutally honest and unaffectionate. It doesn't matter what your pattern has been; all that matters is what you want it to become. Your transformation will require confronting those norms within yourself. Many times breakthroughs can be directly connected to our pushing ourselves out of our comfort zone and into the consciousness that some of the leaks we have in our souls are a result of what we feel we missed at home.

My mother never sat me down and taught me how to say certain things. My father didn't give me a pen and paper to show me how to string words together. Our similarities are directly related to what I observed and ultimately emulated while growing up in their household. I am a product of my environment, just as you are of yours. For some this may be affirming; however, for many this can be frustrating. How do you come to terms with being the product of an environment you don't understand or perhaps even detest? Our environment either inspires who we want to become or challenges us on what we must avoid.

Our environment either inspires who we want to become or challenges us on what we must avoid.

What happens when your environment has to shape you into someone you didn't want to become? I spent much of my life trying to avoid being confined to limits of a kid growing up in Christian ministry. I was intimidated by the expectations of Christianity presented in my subculture. I reasoned that ignoring it would be the easiest path for me. I know that we're supposed to be thankful for the life we've been given, but when the life uncovers or creates insecurities, it's difficult to embrace it. Though things haven't always been easy financially, emotionally, or spiritually for my family, there is always an expectation of perfection when you are a part of a ministry family.

When you are shaped by your environment, you search for the best parts of what you've seen to emulate. You judge your life by what you can see of other people's existence. From my vantage point it seemed like everyone in my environment had strong walks with God and unshakable faith, which I was not sure I could even correctly replicate. I was tempted to mimic the outward expressions of faith that surrounded me by being boisterous in prayer and by constantly reciting scripture. Instead, I chose to distance myself completely from the environment that shaped me.

Once you come to a place where you're able to look beyond the surface layer of that environment, you will recognize that the essence of that world has been instilled deeply within you. Taking the time to understand the environment that shaped you is necessary so that you can recognize the inclinations that may exist within you. I have no doubt that there is no one else on the planet like you. When God decided this world needed you, He created a village to surround you, and His presence is ever with you.

Unfortunately, that village is not one we always understand. Sometimes that village can seem to cause more damage than good, and we are left wondering why God would place us in a situation that seems to be detrimental. But consider this: we could be the factor that begins to change our circle for the better.

He placed you in an environment full of nuances, undercurrents, and obstacles that would nurture your purpose in life.

Each component of that environment plays an integral role in fulfilling the original intention He had when creating you. Your childhood circumstances have played an essential role in producing the inner characteristics you need to overcome every obstacle assigned to your life.

Did you know that your obstacles were assigned by God? There's a passage in Jeremiah that tells us God has plans for us. Those plans are meant to prosper us, not to harm us. When those plans are completed, we will receive a future and a hope. It doesn't matter how the early stages of your life began. All that matters is how dedicated you are to pursuing that expected end. There will be moments in your life when you question if your life is full of dead ends, but avoid placing a stop sign where God only placed a yield. Sometimes God has to allow other people to go ahead of you so that the path can be clear when you get there.

Avoid placing a stop sign where God only placed a yield.

Your environment has worked for you, not against you. When you look back at your history, you won't just see the moments you felt like quitting or moments of uncertainty. You should look back on your life with the knowledge that even when you felt as though you could not continue on, God was strengthening you. We may be blank canvases when we're born, but as time goes on, dimensions and layers are added to us and the mystery of God's plan for our lives is revealed. Hopefully some of those layers are worth being proud of, but there are times when those layers create resentment within us.

∽

Through the connection that the World Wide Web affords, I've been fortunate to interact with many people. Albeit not frequent, I occasionally receive a comment that suggests the personal struggles I've faced weren't as intense because of the stability of the home I came from. Those comments remind me that I used to resent the security I had at home because it alienated me from my peers. As a teenager and early in my adulthood, I often distanced myself from the areas of privilege that my parents sacrificed for because I desired the respect that came from building a career and family on my own. My desire to reject that support robbed me of the wisdom and tools that could have made my journey much easier.

Growing Up Jakes

On the outside looking in, our home would have looked like the quintessential family in ministry. As uninformed teenagers, however, my siblings and I did not fully recognize the value of the lifestyle that had been afforded to us. In our minds we saw our parents working so hard that they weren't always available.

When I was born, my parents began receiving government assistance to care for their five children. Providing for a family of seven takes serious hard work. My mother created a home environment that allowed for my father to expand the horizons of his ministry through book publishing, music, television, and film. As his endeavors proved to be successful, those results began to change our lifestyle. My parents went from receiving government assistance when I was a baby to being a source of spiritual, emotional, and often financial support for other people. It seemed gradual at first, but we became accustomed to a surplus where there was once lack. During our crazy teenage years, we didn't realize just how much effort goes into maintaining a stable living situation and providing opportunities for higher learning for five children. We just knew that we wanted our parents to schedule their lives around us. Our inexperience gave us a limited vantage point. Whether my father was producing multimedia content or working three to four jobs to provide for us, his free time was sparse.

There were times when my siblings and I wanted all of the benefits of our parents' hard work without any of the responsibility or practicality that came along with it. We had a vision of what our lives should look like. We wanted the luxury of the finer things in life and didn't recognize the discipline and commitment it required.

In retrospect I realize that feelings of entitlement and perceived superior knowledge made me question decisions my parents made when raising us. It wasn't until I was looking into the eyes of my teenaged son towering over me that I realized how little I knew then.

When my husband Touré and I began blending our two families, four of our six children were already teenagers. There hasn't been a day since when I don't call or at least think about calling my parents to apologize for my blissful ignorance as a teenager. If I had actually known everything I thought I knew, I would have been a much better daughter. I know now that I benefited from my parents' work ethic, focus, precision, and endurance; those became a road map for navigating my purpose.

Very few parents begin their journey with the idea of failure in mind. Almost all of us make a commitment to constantly learn from our mistakes so that we can pass along those lessons to our children. The hope is that the road our children have to take will be much easier because we blazed a trail. We never take into account how many of our own insecurities parenting will bring to the surface. Parenting often means viewing our own issues of abandonment, rejection, and fear of being misunderstood play out in the lives of our children. If we don't take the time to address those concerns, we run the risk of leaving our children powerless against the demons that haunt us.

Life will require that you see your parents not as heroes who let you down but as humans trying to get things right in spite of their own struggles. You'll have to see them the way God sees them, not the way you needed them to be. It will be challenging, but it's the only way to offer forgiveness. Maybe you're dealing with the grief of having an absentee father. What if I told you that your father didn't leave just because he was selfish? He simply had fears that were too daunting to bear. What if I told you that your mother was emotionally unavailable only because no one had been available to her? I don't know what your environment was like, but I know that none of us has had a completely perfect life. Finding the grace to look outside of yourself and at the variables that created the problems in your environment is key to you understanding how you became the person you are.

Your tiny, perfect little body was once nestled in the arms of a parent. Your soul was unscathed by the harsh truths of life. Within minutes a million thoughts about who you would become flooded the mind of the person who would be your guide in life. Doctors and nurses came in and out of the room constantly checking to make sure that your caregiver was comfortable taking care of you. As they guided your entrance into the world and transition into the home, your parents knew that it was time for their role to fully kick in.

"What if I'm not good at this?" "What if I don't know what to do when they cry?" "What if I mess up?" Many insecurities come to the surface when you're raising children. Second-guessing is a constant stop on your train of thoughts. Very few parents are able to fully execute the plan of transparency and vulnerability with their children. Determining what to say, how much to share, and when to say it is a constant struggle.

Reading books, watching videos, and sharing experiences help, but any good advice is contingent on whether we're able to suspend our personal issues. These resources tell us that unattended children crave attention that often leads to devastation. Then they say that overly attentive parents create self-centered children. No matter where on the spectrum you were raised, you're bound to have experienced some errors when your parents were raising you.

It's hard to believe when you're a teenager that your parents are often just as ill-equipped to handle life's unexpected circumstances as their children. My husband and I call our teenagers "adults in training." We feel it is our job to help them exercise morality, responsibility, and strategy regarding their lives. It is our prayer that they listen intently to what we say and apply it to their lives. However, we realize that there will be some things they must learn the hard way.

It's not until parents begin experiencing adolescent emotional outbursts or rebellious behavior that the disconnects are revealed. If those disconnects are never confronted and healed, then we become adults full of words we never said and emotions we never processed. The ability to disconnect within and avoid discovering the root of our emotions creates a complicated life.

If you don't have any children, you're probably thinking, *All of this is great, but what does it have to do with me?* This topic is important for you to understand because adolescence is the gateway to adulthood. Much of what you understand socially and emotionally occurred in your teenage years. You're likely to uncover incredible things that remind you of the generational strength and wisdom that is available to you, but you may also find pills that are difficult to swallow. My goal is to give you perspective on how your family structure may be responsible for the recurring themes in your life. You can have peace knowing that just because life started one way doesn't mean it has to end that way.

My husband and I have been praying to have the most success in helping our children form a proper mental paradigm to tackle the issues of life. Our answers to their questions are important, but what weighs more heavily is what we demonstrate for them to observe every single day. At a time when their ideas on faith, love, friendship, and family are being shaped, there is no better guide for a child than the blueprint of their parents' journey.

We can all think of an area in our lives where we feel our parents may have dropped the ball. Because we take for granted that which we've always had access to, it's human nature to focus on what we did not receive. The reality is that lamenting about what you didn't get doesn't change that you didn't receive it. Ignoring what your parents were able to offer, no matter how little it was, devalues the gift that it was. We must come to a place in our faith walk where we have so much trust in God's divine plan for our lives that we are encouraged by what we experienced as a teen. Confidence in God's plan helps us to draw the conclusion that if we did not receive something it is because we did not need it.

I pray that one of those things our children learn is that we did the very best we knew how to do with the family God blessed us with. Whether your family was perfectly constructed or undeniably fractured, the people in your life did the best they could. You may be thinking, *Well, that wasn't enough!* I'm telling you it was. Some parents are dealing with insecurities so great that all they can do is self-sabotage anything or anyone that comes close to them. You have to come to a place where you forgive your parents for not providing everything you needed.

Life has a way of slowly stripping away our hope and innocence. Lack of attention, surviving rejection by our peers, facing difficulty in school, grief, bullying, financial instability, and so many more challenges can harden us. Recognizing that those difficult moments not only hurt us in life but also prepared us for life is almost unfathomable. Taking the next step and choosing to believe that those same disappointing moments serve to make your life better takes unyielding faith because pain is a teacher that every soul learns to respect.

Ruth's Family History, Interrupted

One of the stories in the Bible that I've always found fascinating is about a woman named Ruth. The environment that shaped her was a town called Moab. Idolatry was prevalent in that region. When Ruth married her husband, she converted to his religion, Judaism, and became a part of his family. Ruth converted to his religion at the expense of having to separate from the familiarity of the environment she knew.

Ruth's new family included her husband's parents, brother, and a sister-in-law. Unfortunately one by one the men in her new family died, including her husband. All that was left was her mother-in-law and sister-in-law. After the passing of her sons and husband, Ruth's mother-in-law, Naomi, set out to return to her hometown of Bethlehem. Naomi urged Ruth and her sister-in-law to stay in Moab where they had friends and family to comfort them. Though her sister-in-law caved, Ruth could not be coerced to go back to the way things were.

Ruth journeyed with Naomi back to Bethlehem. There Ruth began providing for them by gleaning barley in a nearby field. When she returned from her first day of work in the fields, Naomi could not believe how much barley Ruth had collected. When Naomi learned that Ruth was working in a field owned by a man named Boaz, she rejoiced. Boaz was kin to Naomi's former husband. When Ruth's and Naomi's husbands passed away, they lost connection to any family who could help them reestablish themselves. That was, until Ruth connected with Boaz. Boaz could marry Ruth and not just protect and cover her, but also improve both Ruth and Naomi's lifestyle. He was what the Bible refers to as their kinsman redeemer. A kinsman redeemer restores or preserves the full community rights of disadvantaged family members.

Ruth could have allowed the bitterness of not having the family she desired consume her, but instead she chose to remain hopeful that God had a plan.

As a match needs friction to produce a flame, the challenges you've faced are the friction you need to produce a light that shines for the world to see. For many reasons I believe that Ruth's tenacity and integrity led to the breakthrough she experienced for her family. When Ruth converted to Judaism in Moab, she had to risk being uncomfortable in a place that was once so familiar to her. At that time her community knew only one version of her. As she pursued the desires of her heart, parts of her became foreign. As you embark on this journey, the first people who will notice are those who've been in your environment the longest. You'll have to withstand the pressure to live dual lives and instead risk the isolation that comes with changing your life. Ultimately it was Ruth's difference that made her stand out to Boaz. She embarked on a life of discomfort and far exceeded what she could have ever imagined for her life. Don't be so locked in to what everyone else around you thinks you should become that you limit the destiny on your life.

Think about Boaz's role in this story. I have to admit that for the longest time I felt that Ruth was the star because of her demonstration of steadfast faith. But think of the true power of Boaz as the kinsman redeemer. He could have decided that there were some dilemmas too broken in his family to even attempt fixing them. He could have chosen to ignore his family and create a life that distanced him from them completely. Instead he took ownership of his ability to create change, and through his union with Ruth kings would be birthed. In fact, Matthew named Ruth in the lineage of Jesus! So where would we be without Boaz?

As a match needs friction to produce a flame, the challenges you've faced are the friction you need to produce a light that shines for the world to see.

Your commitment to searching your heart, learning your patterns, and learning from your family positions you to be the kinsman redeemer your family needs. You can restore the emotionally and spiritually disadvantaged members of your family by simply demonstrating and facilitating an introduction to the power of vulnerability. Attempts at trying to control the people in your life are futile, but you can control how you receive and understand them. There are times when we can be so consumed with wanting to change the people in our lives that we don't always ask God to show us how people became the way they are. When we have been wronged, our hearts become hardened and we only see people through the broken fulfillment of hopes we had. That hardness doesn't just make us jaded toward them. It jades our outlook on the world as a whole. Forgiveness is obtained when we release people from the obligation to live up to the expectation we had at the time they hurt us. When we see people's decisions through their brokenness and not ours, we're able to be more empathetic. Empathy doesn't erase hurt, but it does make it easier to digest.

When we begin to address and overcome our insecurities, we give other people permission to do the same. Your children's children will be affected by your decision to demonstrate the power of breaking unhealthy patterns in your family. You will spark a change that shifts your family in the direction of healing for generations to come, all because you started to work on yourself first.

5

Frienemies

Were we best friends because we brought out the best in each other or were we just the best at making the most of being broken? How could I have guessed that loving me would mean losing you? We made a vow to stick through it all together, but I don't think we ever considered the toll that growth would take on us. You were the person I thought would always be in my corner no matter how bad things got, but when things became better for me, your voice grew silent and our connection went from lukewarm to cold. Now all that's left are the words neither of us can say and the emotions we can't ignore. Nothing happened. There was no argument or breaking point. Just a fork in the road that forced us to choose: Would we stay bitter together or become better alone? I couldn't wait for your decision so I began to blaze my own trail. At first I could see you still standing at the fork in the road staring at me. I could even hear your voice as you pondered what was best for you. But with each step I took, your image became hazy until all that was left was a silhouette. I can't connect with you unless I'm willing to go back to who I used to be. I made a vow to God to move to wherever He *says I'm supposed to go. Some good-byes are harder than others; the ones we don't see coming are the ones that sting the most. I don't know if this is good-bye forever, my friend, but it's certainly "See you later."*

Remember the playground promises made on swings? Back then trust came easy and forgiving came down to an exchange of fruit snacks. You could have never told us then that friendships that last for a lifetime are easier to find on television than reality.

I can remember when a pinky promise and a cookie split down the middle equated to a covenant of lifelong friendship. I can remember moments of instantaneous bonding on the first day of school. Sometimes it only took a few short months before I realized that those promises of forever friendships had expiration dates. It's difficult to believe in the moment that the bonds you forge in friendship could ever be broken, but it happens.

Like the seasons that come and go, so are the people assigned to our lives to help us endure certain periods.

Little by little small things begin to add up. Questions begin to form in your mind that distance you from fully connecting the way you once did. One can't help but wonder, "What happened to us?" Friendships that I thought would last forever disintegrated as the ebbs and flows of life revealed shaky foundations. In a way I became fond of the shakiness. I knew that regardless of how large our arguments were we'd take some time to cool off and be laughing or joking about something soon enough. But you can't continue to hurl darts at each other before one cuts too deep. A joke too far, an argument too heated and that friendship ends.

Other friendships don't end so much as they fade away. No major moment of conflict occurs, just a graduation, a marriage, a move . . . and time causes us to grow apart. We learn not to promise forever friendships. Like the seasons that come and go, so are the people assigned to our lives to help us endure certain periods.

Are Your Friendships Worth Keeping?

The best way to determine whether or not the friendships you have are worth it is to determine if they are benefits or detriments. Are they friends of convenience or friends worth investing in?

Shared Flaws and Fears

Was your friendship created from having similar anxieties, fears, or insecurities? Friendships built on insecurities have the potential to produce more uncertainty in your life. Paying careful attention to your friendships is important because friends can and will see you in and advise you during your most vulnerable moments. The person you call friend will be the sounding board you trust to guide and navigate your life.

It's imperative to remember that just because someone was with you through a hard time doesn't mean he or she will be with you for a long time. One of the hardest parts of growing up is learning to let people go. Hanging on to the idea of who you think someone is does not do any favors to yourself or that person. You will have to let go of people you never thought would leave your side. You will notice trends and patterns in them that are detrimental to your well-being. Recognizing that a person's pro-clivities and tendencies are a reflection of who you are may force you to make some difficult decisions.

Life Circumstances That Test Friendships

Becoming a mother at an early age made me grow up quickly. When other children my age were focused on homecoming and school sporting events, I was trying to potty train my child. Our focuses were so different that our conversations had strict limits. Outside of schoolwork or a few television shows, there was very little to discuss with other kids my age. Sometimes your life experiences will keep you from fitting into the circles closest to you. There is a loneliness that comes with being different. If not embraced with the proper mind-set, your need to feel connected will make you resent the circumstances that created the isolation in the first place. I had to come to a place where I realized maintaining certain friendships would only yield eventual disappointments. I knew that having friends who place value on the ability to go out frequently or indulge in youthful spontaneity would not be for me. My time was limited and getting out of the house created strategy.

Friendship is so much greater than sharing interests. There are anywhere from hundreds of thousands to millions of people who share your hobby. Literature, film, music, arts, and crafts are all decorations for friendship. The core of friendship is a deep understanding of who the person you're engaging is. In the best circumstances they will be wise counsel. Their opinions will only lead you back to a place of centering with God. They won't encourage you to stay in situations that increase your dysfunction. They'll be sensitive when you need to make decisions on your own, but honest when asked for their advice. You need people around you who only see you at your best even when life is throwing all kinds of problems your way. There will be times when you need to vent and they can be an ear without judging. True friends do not boast in either joy or judgment when they see you in your weakest moments. Instead, friendship should serve as shelter from the storms that life is promised to bring.

When you have encounters with true friends, you feel both humbled and empowered to do what's right. I know from experience, though, that what we need is not always what we desire. There are times when someone encourages us in our anger and helps us to plot our revenge. This offers temporary satisfaction because we feel understood, but yields more long-term conflict than we had before. We inadvertently become loyal to people who serve as outlets for our mutual frustrations, but intimidated by those who challenge us to rise above. When those emotions cease to exist, we're left with the reality that there wasn't enough substance in the friendship to outlast the frustrating, yet temporary life situation.

"Reality" Television

During the eight-week recovery after having my daughter Ella, I was waited on hand and foot. There's a part of me that wants to tell you that having to sit down or nap every time my newborn did was the bane of my existence, but I'd be lying. I enjoyed the unlimited television time, nonjudgmental snacking, and constant rest. The moment my husband left for meetings I would click open the DVR menu to skim through the commercial-free programs that awaited me.

I indulged in all of the reality television drama my sleep-deprived heart desired. I often sat watching with my mouth agape in disbelief. I couldn't believe some of the things that were said. I watched moment after moment of conflict between friends. I began to wonder if some of the friendships were genuine or if they'd simply been produced for entertainment purposes. As I wondered how these "real" people could subject themselves to such rancid behavior without any detectable decorum, it dawned on me why the shows were experiencing so much success. Those shows are successful because people can see glimpses of themselves or people they know.

While it may seem incomprehensible to subject yourself to relationships that obviously carry high levels of drama and dysfunction, the truth is that the shared commonality of the personalities is the platform their shows created. They had a lot in common. Desperate to be understood, we settle for less-than-ideal connections because there is an opportunity to relate. The desire to have your circumstances validated by another is a gateway that leads to begging for friendships that may poison your destiny.

It's difficult to walk away from friendships that once comforted you but have begun restricting you. Humans don't adjust well to change. We prefer a level of consistency and routine reliability in our relationships. It helps when we feel as though we know what we're getting. There's something comforting about believing someone will remain who they've always been. Many parts of you may stay the same, but the prayer is that you'll continue to shed old skin so that you can be renewed and emerge in life with better expectations and perspective. When a person is committed to only one version of who you are, your evolution will create relationship tension.

There will come a point on this journey when you begin to understand that you've created intimate connections with people who are attracted to your dysfunction and therefore can only remain loyal as long as you stay there. It's not a knock on them, but simply a reality you must face. We love to see how imperfect people are. The popularity of reality television is a testament to the comfort we receive when we realize that even people with fabulous lifestyles have ordinary drama. Their dysfunction makes us comfortable with our own mess. Some of the stories that are displayed on our television screens are almost unfathomable. I've got some news for you. It may seem a little difficult to believe at first, but just stick with me; it will all make sense in the end.

We've all had friendships in our lives with people who aided and abetted in our fun and sometimes reckless behavior. As those moments space out and become fewer and far between, the connection that was once so strong begins to fade. It can be hurtful to watch those friendships dissipate, but it is necessary. Naturally you will question how someone who made a promise to be with you forever could walk away so easily. Walking away is a process. The final step is actually leaving, but long before your feet move, your heart and mind begin packing up their bags. In order for you to have peace about the ending, there are things you must understand.

The End of a Friendship

I recently experienced the loss of a friendship I had honestly thought would last forever. The first few days we went without talking, I believed we just needed time to regroup and gather our thoughts. As those days turned to weeks and weeks to months, I realized that something irreparable had happened between us. In the past one of us would have reached out, but I don't think that either of us had that notion. As I reflected on the breakdown of our connection, I was left with many conclusions.

I believe in many ways that we'd become so dependent on each other that we were hindering each other's growth. There were times when we should have been taking things to God in prayer, but instead we placed too much trust in each other's counsel. As a result, we found ourselves constantly seeking validation and affirmation from each other rather than searching for signs from and time with God.

Further examination revealed that our friendship had an intimacy that kept us from being completely vulnerable in our romantic relationships. We were never forced to fully express ourselves to our partners. If we waited long enough, we could find a pocket of time to sneak away from the busyness of our lives to discuss our hurts and issues. For so long we'd become each other's safe haven that when we actually had healthy romantic relationships, we were unable to fully exercise and strengthen the communication required to maintain those bonds.

I had to remind myself over and over again that the demise of the friendship did not make either of us wrong. Sometimes we can live in a culture so obsessed with black or white situations that we fail to fully embrace the reality of gray areas. In my immaturity I wanted to be the victim and vilify the other person so that I could feel better about myself. You don't need a villain to run away from fruitless friendships or relationships, just a sense that avoidable and detrimental distractions will inevitably prohibit you from fulfilling your potential.

Loyalty

As I sorted through the many unhealthy, yet comforting issues that came as a result of our friendship, it dawned on me that loyalty is dependent on many variables. I think we can all agree that one of the most valuable traits any person can hold is loyalty. Webster's defines *loyalty* as "unswerving in allegiance." Before you can determine whether a person is capable of going the long haul with you in a friendship, determine what part of you they're swearing allegiance to.

Loyalty comes in many different shapes and sizes, but there are three aspects of loyalty that I want to focus on in this chapter. The first classification is for people who are loyal to your position. You have encounters with people who are more loyal to your accomplishments than they are to your character. Their association with you affords them a validation about their own standing in social settings. There's a difference between being proud of who someone is and proud of what they have. Loyalty based on your position is dangerous because the one constant promise of life is change.

People who are loyal to your position will leave your circle when your life shifts. We often hear people questioning whether someone could stay connected to them even if their lives changed and they lost their position. While this is something worth considering, there is another perspective that is not often discussed.

It's what happens when your position creates expansion in your life. Often people are loyal to your struggle, so the moment you begin to master your struggle and become more comfortable with the pace and design of your life, they no longer deem themselves valuable. Their feelings of inadequacy cause them to sabotage their friendship with statements that isolate their experience from yours.

The familiar phrase "it's lonely at the top" does not mean people at the top don't want company. Rather, the higher one climbs, the more it reveals the tenacity and fear of those their climbing with. Not everyone will be able to make this climb to self-discovery and ultimate fulfillment with you. When life repositions you, don't be surprised when you begin to notice strains on relationships that once required no effort.

Other people may be loyal to your presentation. These people believe they're being loyal to you, but they're actually loyal to the person you've been pretending to be. I've said it once and I'll say it again: the most dangerous words in any woman's vocabulary are "I'm okay." These words are a sure sign that we are anything but okay! Still, people who don't get a glimpse beyond the masks we wear may not recognize that those words are not always our truth. Their ignorance to that truth makes them loyal to someone who does not truly exist.

The truth is it can be difficult to build genuine friendships when we aren't genuinely in touch with who we are. Until we have an understanding of how we've come to act and think the way that we do, the relationships we create can only be surface level at best. Some people are loyal only to the version of you that is carefree and sometimes even reckless. This is difficult to believe because we often expect people to make their intentions clear by wearing them on their sleeves. But most people aren't aware enough of their own sharp edges to warn you that they exist. It's not until you begin to shed the excuses that limit your potential that you recognize the holes in their character that ultimately create dysfunction in your life.

There's no way to fully determine whether a person is truly interested in investing in you until you've invested in yourself. Losing the comfort of relationships that provide entertainment but no substance requires maturity and discipline. Television is for entertainment; life is about growth. You can't allow the desire to be accepted to keep you from fully accepting yourself.

Lastly, the best type of loyalty comes from a friend who is loyal to who you are. Before we dive into this type of person it's important to remember that people can be loyal to who you are, but that does not mean they'll be present to watch you come into full maturation. Loyalty is not just about presence; it's about allowing a person to evolve and grow. In its purest state loyalty is a commitment to protecting another's reputation, evolution, and heart while expecting nothing in return. Loyalty is not about how it benefits the other person; rather, it has everything to do with a personal commitment to being a quality person. So often we confuse loyalty and longevity. Loyalty is not a promise to always be around; in fact, loyalty is best proven when two people are not around. It is when one person lives in such a way that nothing will happen on their watch that could hurt you later. Loyalty does not die when a friend is not around. Loyalty should never be contingent on proximity. Whether time passes and friendship fades or a rhythm has been created that allows for comfort, there are principles that should remain intact regardless.

After You Take Your Inventory

There is one major benefit that comes with taking inventory of your life. It helps you to qualify what type of relationships you need and which ones you must sacrifice. The relationships we choose to keep and invest in reflect how we see ourselves. Many of us have friends who give us permission to be bitter, angry, and lost. You've heard the saying "misery loves company," but have you considered fully what that means? I know when I've heard it I've always thought that it never applied to me because my life wasn't completely miserable. I had enough pockets of joy and fulfillment that I considered myself to be pretty balanced. It wasn't until I stopped masking my hurt and pain that I came to terms with the fact that there were moments in my life that were more than miserable; they were devastating. The devastation allowed me to bond with people I thought of as "friends" over broken hearts and lowered standards.

One of the hardest parts about evolving is recognizing when the foundation of some of your most valued friendships is superficial material. The idea of lifelong friendships sounds great in theory, but they require a level of parallel maturity and growth that doesn't often happen. In my own lifetime I've experienced the loss of treasured friendships. It has made me recognize the role I played and the errors I made. At times I've found myself speechless after realizing that our evolving journeys and different issues had completely robbed me of the comfort that particular friendship once offered. But knowing a friendship that has come to an end was unhealthy doesn't necessarily numb you from the pain.

As you begin to change your life and demand to become better, you'll have to be willing to let a few people go too. You may not be able to wait for the next point of contention. You may have to choose to let your focus on yourself serve as a notice. Eventually your growth will either inspire change or reject everything that insists on staying the same. The separation will be painful, but it will be a necessary component for you to move forward.

Don't allow the fear of confrontation to keep you from discovering deeper dimensions of yourself.

I hope that the realization that you will have to separate yourself from some social circles does not convince you that growth is too expensive. Many times we have to choose between staying under the radar and not causing any tension or friction within our circles or making the bold move to stand on our own. Don't allow the fear of confrontation to keep you from discovering deeper dimensions of yourself. It's okay to let go of one season so that you can live in another. The cycles of life will allow for some relationships to be with us for years while others we may have to release. While some separations may necessitate a good-bye, there are others that will fade away organically as you begin to walk and speak in the consciousness of your truth. You must constantly create conversation that represents your authenticity. As you choose to consistently have that level of transparency, your friendships will begin to reflect that. That reflection may come through separating from those who don't fit those ideals.

6

Forgive and Remember

It seemed like all I ever wanted was to prove I was better than the way you treated me. I wanted the satisfaction of knowing that the tables would turn and life would prove you were wrong about me or, at least, I was right to believe in you. I invested so much of my essence into imagining what actions those feelings would produce if they lived in your chest. Could you finally give me the opportunity I had been praying for? So much time wasted on you that I never took the time to examine my heart. The truth is you hurt me. You hurt me more than I ever wanted to admit. I played tough and wanted to pretend like your words and actions didn't brand my tough exterior with rejection and bitterness, but the poison seeped in. Now all I can wonder is who I would have been had I never let my expectations distort the reality of who you have always been. I see your true colors shining through now and I've made the difficult decision to not let them blind me any longer. No, not this time. I will take those colors in with all of their crazy, beautiful, ugly tones because I know the only way forward is to release you so that I can unleash me.

The rage built like fire in my chest. The pain spilled over like boiling water scorching my hopes and desires. I tasted the bitterness in my mouth and smiled. I was angry. I was hurt. I felt broken beyond repair. I imagined those who hurt me walking away as if nothing had happened while I was left to pick up the pieces of my brokenness. The thoughts running rampant in my head were a vivid reminder of every painful decision that led me into this disaster. I made internal promises of vendettas and vengeance that would serve as a lesson to all who crossed me. When I was finished, everyone around me would be reminded to never attempt to do anything remotely similar ever again. I was far from thinking about what Jesus would do. *I'm not Him*, I thought to myself. *I'm human and this hurts! I can't continue to be walked over like a doormat and still smile as if nothing happened.* I could feel dark thoughts making their permanent home in my mind. No longer was I daydreaming about the possibilities of joy and happiness in my own life. I was thinking of creative ways to reciprocate the damage done to my soul. If I shared even a portion of those schemes with you, I'm afraid your eyes would widen with disbelief, but trust me when I tell you that this girl has not always been so hopeful and optimistic. Quite to the contrary, I've had my share of pain and struggle that has left me with the desire to become a villain in the lives of those who broke me.

Unforgiveness will transform you from victim to the villain. I had to come to the realization that my need to hold accountable the person who hurt me was prohibiting me from seeing the role I played in perpetuating my hurt. At the root of unforgiveness is the hurt we experience by the uncontrollable actions of another. In the haze of whatever has occurred we cannot escape the feeling that we've lost a commodity so precious it cannot be restored. The inability to regain our time, energy, innocence, or investment can grieve us so deeply that we lose all prospects for positive outcomes.

My Models of Forgiveness

I placed my parents in some situations that produced a few gray hairs on my mother's head and may even have been responsible for my father's complete loss of hair. Now that I have children I understand just how exciting a child I must have been to raise. No one likes predictability, right? I kept my parents on their toes like ballerinas. They probably have a permanent tiptoe in their stride. While I can easily tell you about a few things I did that would test even the most patient parents' faith, what's important here is how my parents consistently responded to my decisions: with forgiveness.

That forgiveness did not come without stipulations for regaining trust or having to face the disappointing expressions on their faces. Still, it only took a few awkward encounters after my shenanigan was discovered for us to get back to normal. Their practice of forgiveness taught me to not hold grudges. Because I have been forgiven so many times, it's easier for me to forgive.

There was a crucial component of my parents' forgiveness pattern that I did not recognize as well as I do now. My parents did not allow my mistakes to alter their commitment to me as their child, but they also did not continue on as if nothing happened. "Forgive and forget" makes for a nice slogan, but it's actually no way to live life. In fact, it's impossible. You can't erase the feelings and emotions connected to moments in your life that caused you to question yourself and others in deep ways. Still, there's a fine line between forgive and remember and unforgiveness.

When we are in environments that praise our ability to be mean, spiteful, and bitter toward people, it stunts our growth. When you dwell in the land of unforgiveness, the only people you attract to your life are those who are comfortable with the same mind-set as you. I believe that in many ways forgiving other people comes down to us discovering the most powerful thought.

If you can recognize that people hurt you—whether intentionally or unintentionally—because of their own brokenness, you will begin to have a level of empathy toward them. That empathy does not remove the pain they caused you, but it does help you release them. It has been said over and over again that "hurt people hurt people," which is true, but consider how our own pain blinds us from seeing others' pain. We are often so desperate for validation from someone that we fail to see their humanity. When we imagine someone is incapable of having human failures, we are bound to be disappointed. Many times people hurt me because I had an expectation for them that was rooted in my own desires, not their reality. Therefore my inability to forgive was because they disappointed the role I needed them to fill.

I want to share a story with you about a mother and daughter who experienced this very thing.

"She's always thought she was so much better than everyone," Melanie heard her mother whisper at the dinner table. She was home from the "big city." She was the first one to graduate in her family and instead of coming back to join the family business, she'd decided on a career in New York City. Hoping to relieve the tension that was building in the room, Melanie began cleaning up the kitchen. As she scraped the dishes into the trash and washed away the remaining food that stuck to the plate, a tear sprang from her eye and journeyed down her cheek. The tears came slowly at first, but then more steadily. Afraid that someone would walk in on her red eyes and dripping nose, she scurried to the restroom to get herself together.

The lock on the bathroom door had barely clicked before Melanie's back was pressed against the wall. She slid down to the floor cradling her wet face in her hands. She hated that no matter how old she was or what she accomplished, her mother could still bring her to this point. This wasn't her first time locked in a room of her childhood home. The house had become a prison to her. The mere thought of coming back made anxiety explode inside of her. *All I have to do is survive until tomorrow,* she thought.

Melanie and her mother, Juliet, had a complicated relation-ship. Her mother was always so hard on her, but she could never fully understand why. She was far from a perfect child, but she strived to always seek her mother's validation. It was as though nothing she did was ever good enough in her mother's eyes. She competed in track and broke almost every record her school had. If she were not so determined to be an engineer, she would have pursued becoming an Olympian. Melanie gradu-ated at the top of her class with high honors. She was offered a full scholarship to her first choice. While everyone in her high school senior class was torn between leaving their parents or pursuing their lives, she had been mentally packing her bags since middle school. Graduation was the moment she'd spent years dreaming of; she could remember it like it was yester-day. After an emotional good-bye with her teachers and friends,

Melanie headed home to bid adieu to family. She hugged her little brother tight as he towered over her. She made him vow to carry on the legacy of the family name in high school. One look at her father revealed that he was doing the best he could to keep from breaking down. With a pat on the shoulder and a long, knowing stare, he sent his one and only daughter out into the world. She knew that their moment, though short, would be all that he could handle. But it was more than enough for her. She never had to wonder where she stood with him. Since childhood they always had the uncanny ability to communicate without saying a word. His stare was a nod of support. It was a reminder to her that no matter what she faced while she was away that he was only a call away. Before words could escape her lips, her father scurried upstairs pretending to have work to do. She smiled on the inside because she knew that he did not want her to see him emotional and begin to question her decision to move so far away.

Then there was Juliet. Melanie hoped that this good-bye would expose a version of her mother that she'd never seen. She tried to push back the images of her mother finally embracing her tearfully and telling her how much she loved her. As predictions of what their good-bye would look like played over and over again in her head, she searched through the house for her mother. Melanie found her holding the refrigerator door open while taking ingredients out for dinner. Melanie's voice was barely audible when she uttered the words, "Mom, I'm heading out now." Her mother continued staring into the refrigerator hardly paying her any attention at all. Melanie shuffled her feet hoping to rouse her mother out of her trance. Juliet rolled her eyes and sighed. She closed the refrigerator door and then allowed the words to spew out of her mouth like daggers, "You know you never really knew how to just disappear. Don't think this is going to be some Lifetime movie moment. I know how you've been waiting for this day. Go ahead. Get out! Go start your big fancy life away from us regular people!" Melanie had too much pride to let her mother see the water brimming in the corners of her eyes. She turned her back on her mother and headed out the door.

That was more than six years ago.

She'd only returned home now to bury her father after a sudden heart attack had taken from her the only parent she felt truly loved her. Rising from the cold linoleum floor of the upstairs bathroom, Melanie could hear her brother's voice beginning to rise as he searched for her. Their paths collided at the top of the stairs. He looked at her red face and hugged her just as he did that day when she hopped in her car and took off. Once the house emptied out and all the food was put away, Melanie walked to her bedroom. Just when she was about to close the door, she could hear the soft sobs of her mother coming from down the hall. She tiptoed up to the door quietly. As she peeked through the cracked door, she saw her mother's face buried in one of her father's work shirts. Her mother was always so poised and graceful, but the person she was staring at was far from that. She was a woman stricken with grief. Melanie began to back away from the door, but the floor creaked announcing her presence to her mother.

Juliet looked at her through tear-stained eyes and beckoned for her to come closer. In that moment the two women her father loved the most were both aching, but incapable of consoling each other. They sat there like that, silently staring at each other for what felt like hours, but could have been only a few minutes. Her mother broke the silence and spoke first. It started as a whisper, but as she cleared her throat, it became clearer. "You know . . . it used to bother me how much he talked about you. It was as if the sun and the moon all shined through your eyes. You would walk into the room and I could tell it was the highlight of his day. We had a great marriage, we did. I know that he loved me and God knows I loved him. We had plenty of good times and all, but it hurt like hell to see how he adored you."

This was it. This was the moment Melanie prayed for but was never sure would actually happen. Her father's presence was no longer able to hide the elephant that had always taken up so much space in this small house. Careful to not say anything that would cause the moment to take a turn for the worse, but dying to finally have the answer to the question she'd wanted to ask since adolescence.

"Is that why you hate me so much?" she finally asked.

"Hate you? I could never hate you, Melanie!" she said, clutching her daughter's hands. "You are everything I ever wanted to be. Every time I look at you I'm reminded of the dreams I placed on hold to support this family. You were only in middle school when you started mocking my attempts at helping you with your homework. Each time you won on that track it was a reminder of how stagnant I'd become. I suppose my distance felt like hate, but honestly it was . . . it was much deeper than that. You made me feel ashamed of who I've become."

The truth was unleashed in that room with raw vulnerability and abandoned pride. For years Melanie had been trying to figure out when the divide with her mother began. The truth is that it was created long before Melanie even came into the picture. Juliet was unable to fully celebrate the victories of Melanie's life or withstand the ebbs and flows of teenage attitudes because she never learned to deal with her own disappointments. Instead of seeing the value in the work she invested into creating a family unit and harmonious household, she allowed others' achievements—specifically her daughter's—to taunt her. As a result, Melanie never received the support she felt she needed and became bitter toward her family. The inability to express downfalls in relationships create dysfunction that very gradually turns into resentment. Resentment is a symptom of unforgiveness.

When two parties have resentment, they must both possess an equally powerful resolve to bring resolution. Melanie and Juliet were presented with a unique opportunity to see a vantage point that was only accessible through transparent communication. Juliet's underlying issue of shame and discontent had nearly destroyed her relationship with her daughter. Though they both had the best of intentions, what mattered most was not what they meant but what they did. There are people in your life who you've learned to live around but not with. You are able to be in the same room and tolerate each other, but your issues have created division in your inner circle and there are holes in your soul as a result. If making amends is not feasible, then you must make the decision to embark on a solo journey of forgiveness.

You have to understand that people do the best they can and sometimes their best is hurtful to you. People who do bad things are not always evil; often they are broken. Wouldn't it be nice if connecting with people came with instructions? You'd know exactly how to control your interaction with them and the side effects of having them in your life. Too bad that's only a wish. It is not until you actually begin to know a person that you learn where their fault lines lie. You cannot allow someone's issues to become your stumbling block. Do not become so distracted with trying to diagnose someone's issue that you fail to pursue treatment for your wounds.

We make a mistake when we allow our ability to forgive to be contingent on whether we receive closure from the other person. Closure is not a moment between two people; it is the moment you stop reliving your history and let go of the "what ifs." It is embracing that every ounce of pain you experienced was necessary for your growth and the ultimate setup for your peace and joy. Closure is never about another person. It is reconciliation with one's self.

> *Closure is not a moment between two people; it is the moment you stop reliving your history and let go of the "what ifs."*

While the moment in the story about Melanie and Juliet was powerful, imagine how much healthier it could have been had Melanie not needed something from her mother. What if she'd come to a place within herself where a conversation between the two of them was an added layer of healing, but not the origin of it. I am offering to you an opportunity to cease punishing your emotional assailant with thoughts that lessen your character. You may be thinking, *Because they hurt me, I can't move forward.* You must confront the illegitimacy of such thoughts. You may not feel as though you can move forward, but the truth is you're doing just that! Time is passing you by, days are drifting away, life is moving at full speed, and you don't just get to stand still in the midst of that. Your life is moving forward whether your heart and mind come along with it or not. Taking care of your soul in the midst of the fleeting nature of time is pivotal to overcoming.

A part of that treatment is coming to a difficult truth. Many of us struggle to understand that experiencing failures, hurt, and disappointment has been necessary so that we could confront our own strength. You have not been broken beyond repair. No one walked away with anything you invested in them that cannot be restored. You will look back on the situations that fractured you in life and thank God they occurred. Any satisfaction you're tempted to receive from vengeance masquerades as peace, but it is not until those feelings fade that you realize the ache that began within you is still very much alive.

There are many signs of unforgiveness. I think one of the most obvious is that secret sense of joy we experience when we hear that the people who caused us to stumble are now struggling themselves. Or even one step further, we begin to wish bad things on them so that they can suffer the same way we did. Wishing those types of complications on someone means you have allowed feelings of hurt, vendetta, and revenge to live within you and control your thoughts. Those feelings are rooted in anger and embarrassment. When those feelings live inside of you, they become toxic. That toxicity affects the well-being of your soul. You cannot compartmentalize your hurt. Sooner or later it spreads into every area of your life. That's why it's so important to address every part of your issues.

The emotions and ill will I mentioned in the beginning of this chapter only dissipated when I began to sincerely pray for the people who hurt me. Nothing paralyzes the lips of someone plotting a plan for revenge like asking them to open their mouths and pray for the person who wounded them. When I first began,

my teeth were clenched as if my entire body was trying to revolt.
I realized, however, that the more time I spent focusing on watching the demise of my villain, the less time I had to become my
own superhero. So I said the words:

> *God, You know exactly why I feel the way I do. You know
> the insecurities that played a role in the situation and the
> strength that will come as a result of it. I pray that You
> would help me to see _____ the way that You do. I
> know that at some point they've been hurt and victimized,
> as we all have. I ask that You would begin to heal their
> heart and hurt. Open their eyes to the power they have to
> overcome the things that caused them harm. Help me to
> release them from the pain they caused me. Let us all move
> on and grow from this moment. May the hard-earned lesson
> of this time be a wealth of wisdom for someone else who is
> struggling with the same thing that we're currently facing.
> Bless _____'s heart on this journey that it may be healed
> and restored. In Jesus' name.*

∽

If you're thinking that this book just took a turn in a direction
you're not sure you can handle, it's because you *must* overcome
the feelings that you have buried. When we pray for the people
who've harmed us, we not only become more like Christ, we
become more like ourselves! Reconciling your life is not about
pretending that issues did not affect you. It's admitting the truths
that make you feel your brokenness and regret so that you can

recognize that forward progress only comes by making peace with what has occurred in your past.

Some of us deal with unforgiveness because we are unable to vocalize that any hurt occurred at all. I'm guilty of doing this very thing! I can become so irritated and agitated by the actions of someone, but never ever admit to them that their actions hurt me. People cannot apologize for things they did not know hurt you. Keeping silent to keep from having confrontation does not make conflict disappear; it only creates an environment for it to grow and fester until it eventually becomes unavoidable.

Then, when you finally reach your breaking point, you barrage someone with a list of things they've done wrong; meanwhile they're staring at you with disbelief. There are times when unforgiveness is a process that you have to work through on your own, because you do not have access to the person you have to convince to see their wrong before even getting to the point of forgiveness. Then there are other times when you have well-intentioned people in your life who are trying to love you but are still learning your sensitivities. You cannot penalize them for their ignorance.

Forgiveness may come very easily once you give the person a chance to see how their actions negatively affected you. No matter how perfect a person seems, they are still trying to figure out this thing called life just like the rest of us. It is a mistake to be merciful only to people who have a struggle you can empathize with. True forgiveness can only occur when you make a decision to not see a person for who you want them to be, but see them as another person on this earth learning their way. Once you are armed with that knowledge, the next decision is up to you to make. Whether a person can be in your life after the damage they've caused comes down to the vision you have for your life and if you believe they're a part of that vision. This is when forgive and remember comes into play. Don't become so wrapped up in your forgiveness that you try to give a person chance after chance to your own detriment.

On the contrary, if you have been on the other side of an offense and have caused harm to someone else, you must be willing to give them time to grow. You cannot force someone to forgive you, but your life does not have to be stagnant while they determine whether they can afford to give you another chance. Your character and integrity should never be contingent on someone else's actions. There are times when in lieu of waiting for someone's forgiveness you must choose to forgive yourself and move forward with your life armed with changed behavior.

True forgiveness can only occur when you make a decision to not see a person for who you want them to be, but see them as another person on this earth learning their way.

Maya Angelou once said, "When a person shows you who they are, believe them the first time." If a person has proved that they are not stable or conscientious enough to be an integral part of your life, continuing to engage them is dangerous. Expect to have your life unnecessarily broken when you could be striving toward wholeness. That decision to allow poison to flow unfiltered into your life transfers the role of villain from being an external entity and into the person who stares back at you when you look in the mirror. You can no longer blame them for your tears. No, you must take responsibility for allowing someone who did not understand your worth to determine your value. Forgiving them will still have to take place, but the deeper conversation you must be willing to have is how you forgive yourself.

You cannot punish yourself for relationships that did not live up to your expectations. I hope you forgive yourself for not loving yourself, for not thinking highly enough of yourself to demand the best from and for your heart. I hope you're pacified by the knowledge that you're not the only one who has ever made a choice that made them question themselves later, but I'm praying that you see there is still an opportunity for you to love yourself now. Love is so powerful that even from where you stand now you can learn to love the person you once were. You don't have to separate yourself any longer. You don't have to wish that you had chosen a different path. I can promise you that even in the midst of those moments that God was loving you, just as He is loving you now. You may ask yourself, *How is this possible?* It's because He created the blueprint for forgiveness. He knew that even as you were doing the very thing that hurt you, you were only doing so because you were seeking all of the components of love. The kind of love that 1 Corinthians 13 talks about. "Love is patient, love is kind. It does not envy, it does not boast, it is not proud. It does not dishonor others, it is not self-seeking, it is not easily angered, it keeps no record of wrongs. Love does not delight in evil but rejoices with the truth. It always protects, always trusts, always hopes, always perseveres" (vv. 4–7, NIV).

Shame

When we are able to walk in the forgiveness of God, we are liberated from feelings of shame. The mental barricade that prohibits us from being able to do this is the stained glass of shame that we often view our lives through. Shame is the emotion we have when our actions contradict our essence and reveal or expose insecurities we were not aware that we possessed. Releasing thoughts of shame is part of the process of forgiving yourself. Shame cannot be present where vulnerability did not exist. Choosing to avoid vulnerability does not force shame to dissipate. In fact, it does quite the opposite. It allows the entirety of your life to be controlled by one moment, one decision, one memory. You must choose to stop punishing your destiny because of your history that brings you shame.

It was 2011 when I made a decision to no longer live under the blanket of shame that had begun to dictate my life. After I started a blog on the corner of the Internet that grew to regularly touch the lives of tens of thousands, some members of the conference department of my father's church asked me if I would introduce him at our women's conference, "Woman! Thou Art Loosed." Up until that point I was known for being shy and shrinking whenever anyone would ask me to do something that involved public speaking.

However, this time was different. There was something inside of me that had been comforted by the blog. Each time I posted, I connected with another soul with a totally different life path than my own. In some capacity everyone's story was a reminder to me that the feelings that once isolated me had been felt before by women of all different ages, hues, and socioeconomic backgrounds. That knowledge gave me the confidence to give a voice to the words I could once only write. As I took the stage in front of twenty thousand women, I wanted my story to offer liberty to another woman who felt bound by the decisions she made and experiences she couldn't erase.

From that moment many things in my life began to change. I didn't realize it then, but I know now that that moment gave me permission to begin distracting myself with myself. Up until then my search for forgiveness had become about seeking validation from unhealthy places. Because I was unable to forgive myself, I was also unable to receive forgiveness from other people. When I finally uttered the words from the stage, I was able to finally say, "This is who I am. This is where I've come from. I am evidence that broken crayons still color and there is still life inside of you." While that moment was liberating for me, it also left me feeling completely vulnerable.

You see, when most of your time has been dedicated to shame and self-pity and you make an effort to finally accept yourself, you have to also redirect the energy that was once used to hold yourself down. Now is the time to pull yourself up! You must begin to decide what the dream for your life will be and how you will make decisions that make it a reality. The dream for your life does not have to be a grand scheme to have your name in lights every night. If that's your goal then I challenge you to dig deeper. In the best-case scenario those types of accomplishments are an outward expression of an internal decision you made.

If you're like I was in that season, some of the relationships and opportunities you currently possess in your life are a result of shame. When we ignore unresolved shame, it takes root and produces fruit in our actions. Distracting yourself with rebuilding yourself is a commitment to focusing on areas of your life that are within your grasp to improve.

The most powerful thing you can do is choose to believe that regardless of what has happened to you, you will not allow it to change the goodness inside of you. When I divorced my first husband, I secretly began going to the gym. Until then, taking care of my health was not something I had learned to do. I've never been athletic, and as a girl raised in the South my curvaceous figure never made me feel insecure. I decided to try a healthy, clean-eating, and active lifestyle for a month. I was convinced that the time would be somewhat wasted because I was "supposed" to be thick. After dropping fifteen pounds the first month, it became clear that not only was I capable of losing weight, but I was also capable of taking control of my normal and creating something better.

We only find it difficult to forgive when something occurs that is out of our control. Allowing your emotions to control what you think and believe about people is no way to take care of your heart.

Your character cannot be defined by the actions of someone else. You've survived too much to allow your joy to be based on someone else's affliction. You don't have to forgive and forget to move on. In fact, I encourage you to do just the opposite of forgetting: remember.

Remember what happened to you because it gave you perspective you would have never had otherwise. Remember the insecurities that created hurtful actions in your life so that you can avoid them in the future. Remember that you once felt so broken that you even questioned your sanity. It will help people in similar positions one day to realize they aren't crazy, or maybe they are, but at least they are not the first to have been in that space before.

Your life is the road map that will help other people avoid detours that delay them on their road to manifesting a destiny greater than those moments that have ailed them. Don't throw it away because you don't like the marks that have been made. Fold it neatly, tuck it away in your heart, and preserve its beauty because someone is going to need evidence that even lost people find their way home.

7

Connecting with God

It's taken me all of this time to realize how much I mean to You. I look back on the times when life was breaking me to my core and I see Your love constantly surrounding me. Somehow I let the idea of what our connection was "supposed" to look like rob me of the beauty of what it truly was. I can remember the moments when I felt so connected to everything around me. I remember the moments when life felt so much bigger than me and instead of making me feel afraid, it invigorated me. It made me feel like all things were possible for me. Now that I've hurt a bit more and cried a few more tears, I realize that hope is an endangered emotion in a world full of fear. Yet, You've constantly refilled the jar that holds my hope when I needed it the most. The more I followed the voice within that challenged me not just to feel good, but to be better, the more I realized that voice was You all along. I always felt like there would be this moment when a deep booming voice would grab my attention. I didn't realize it was truly the still small voice that was on the inside of me ordering each of my steps into a direction that would reveal the best of me. Thank You for *preserving me, for keeping me protected, for trusting me with this breath. Now that my eyes have been opened, I see You in everything. I see Your love staring at me in the craziest of moments. It's in the words that find me right when I need them. It's in the way I thought I was down to my last, but I got a second chance right when I needed it. It's in the way You gave me the strength to walk away. It's in the way You gave me the discipline to withstand the pain and process of change. All this time I thought that I wasn't good enough for You, but the truth is You were waiting for me to see that even when I felt the most alone, You've been covering me.*

When I was growing up, people in my church often said that they felt as though they were "God's favorite." Though I would laugh and nod my head, the truth is I never fully understood.

My relationship with God has been complicated. That may sound strange coming from the daughter of a pastor or it may even be expected, given the stereotype that exists about preachers' kids. I just couldn't fully fathom the concept of there being a higher power that had great affection and love for me as an individual.

When I look at the earth, the miracle of birth, and the vast natural wonders that exist, I know undoubtedly that the source of civilization began in the mind of a Master Creator. The barricade that existed for me in my relationship with God was constructed by many false representations of God. Those false ideas derived from experiences in church, low self-esteem, mistakes, and disappointments that produced extreme tension. To put it frankly, I believed in God, but I struggled with the idea that God believed in me. That internal quarrel made it difficult for me to have a personal revelation and relationship with Him.

When the day-to-day frustrations of life begin to pile up, it may be difficult for you to remember, but living in the consciousness of this truth each day will give you perspective on how to navigate circumstances that are out of your control. I have come to the realization that you are more than a body taking up space on this earth. Your life was manifested because of a need that existed in the world. Feelings of unworthiness don't just damage our relationships; they diminish our ability to maximize the power available to us through our divine connection with God.

There is nothing that has ever happened to you or anything that you've done that cannot work to produce peace and joy in your life. If you're like me, you may be thinking about all of the memories that invalidate this thought. I totally understand, but the truth is there is not one incredible thing in my life currently that did not come through the by-product of something that once caused me great pain. From the depths of your sorrow, God wants to manifest blessings that far outweigh any hurt you've experienced. When life becomes tough, we begin to believe that we have been dealt an unfair hand. No matter how much we believe this to be so, we always have encounters with people who are experiencing something worse. When you become so consumed with counting what is going wrong with your life that you don't take the time to truly appreciate what is going well, you invite despair.

Regret obscures the possibilities that exist in the present. You don't get do-overs in life because you don't need them. You needed to mess up. You had to make those mistakes. Your heart had to be broken. You needed to lose your way. There are lessons in those moments that could not have been delivered any other way. You cannot live in the past and maximize the present.

I've got a list as long as the Mississippi of things that have occurred in my life that were less than ideal. With each disappointment and setback I found myself drifting further and further away from the idea that God has a perfect plan for my life. I couldn't understand why He would allow some of the things I experienced to happen to me. As if those thoughts were not tormenting enough, there were the other thoughts that plagued me when I tried to believe in His unconditional love. It was the idea that I'd done too much to receive the redemption I so desperately wanted. Convinced that any hope of better was reserved for those who'd chosen a more righteous past, I created a faith relationship that worshiped God but demeaned myself. You cannot love God and hate your life at the same time. Our greatest responsibility and challenge in the quest for higher thinking is daring to find light in our darkest situations. This can be difficult for those of us who would rather avoid uncovering that darkness altogether. Because we don't believe that anything good can come from the bad we experienced, nothing good comes from the bad we experienced.

Regret obscures the possibilities that exist in the present.

How can we believe in a God that is pro everything else in the world except our lives? I had to be willing to confront my feelings of inadequacies when dissecting my relationship with God. The steps to do that were challenging, but I want to share them with you. I learned some things in the process that I believe can help bring you closer to God.

What My Birthday Taught
Me About God's Love

One of the first birthdays I spent with my husband Touré happened when he was just my boyfriend. Because I was still living in Texas and only visiting him in California, I knew few people in the area, but being as smitten as I was (and still am), I knew that I could not go wrong spending my birthday with him. He managed to gather the handful of people I was acquainted with and some of his close friends to a surprise birthday party for me at a restaurant right by the beach. I was so blown away at the thoughtful gesture. I felt loved and happy.

The following year my birthday fell on a day when we were a few days from moving. I planned to stop the pace long enough to enjoy a nice dinner, but most of my family and friends were still in Texas so I didn't expect much hoopla. Then I looked on the calendar and realized that my birthday was on a Sunday. My husband and I lead an incredible community of believers in the Los Angeles area. Each Sunday we have three powerful worship services. The energy and investment that goes into facilitating those three services can be both powerful and exhausting. I knew that anything we managed to do for my birthday would be secondary to the mission we have for Sunday. To be honest I wasn't upset about that either. You could have never told me that I would come to a place where I did not mind being at church for three services on my birthday. Talk about a transformation! I went from not feeling very special to God to spending one of my most special days in church.

My husband, on the other hand, was not content with the idea of us having a low-key celebration. Touré decided that instead of trying to celebrate on Sunday when we would be tired, we would dedicate the weekend to our celebration. It all began on Friday with an early-morning boating trip. While we were on the water, we witnessed a school of dolphins swimming directly toward us. It was as if he'd convinced the universe to come together to celebrate my existence. We went to see a movie I'd really been wanting to check out, and then our celebration concluded with a good ol' fashioned nap. Saturday I made breakfast for our children, then Touré took me to do some damage at one of my favorite stores because they were having a sale. After dinner with the kids that evening, I was feeling completely celebrated beyond measure. When Sunday rolled around, I was grateful to be in the presence of God and surrounded by believers. I knew that Touré might mention my birthday, but I wasn't prepared for the surprise video tribute he presented. Somehow he'd been working behind the scenes to put together clips from my family, friends, and members of the church all wishing me a happy birthday. I was in tears when my parents' faces appeared on the screen and in a full ugly cry when my son finished sharing his tribute.

To say the least, I was completely and utterly amazed at all the thought and secrecy that must have taken place for Touré to have planned such an incredible moment. I was completely satisfied with the full weekend we'd already experienced, but the video truly put the icing on the cake. Just when I thought things were over after Sunday's services, Touré and I piled our six children into one car and headed for what I thought would be a quiet dinner. When the maître d' walked us to our table, I was greeted by "Surprise!" Our closest friends and family were there. Even my parents had flown in!

Just between us, I was not completely caught off guard. Earlier in the day our sons were arguing over who would get to sit in the front row. One of them mentioned that he would have fair opportunity because of dinner that evening. I continued buckling our infant daughter Ella into the car seat as if I did not hear him spill the beans. Later on in the day one of our teenage daughters hugged us after service then confirmed the time of the dinner within my earshot. Once again, I pretended not to hear because I knew my husband's intentions were for me to be surprised. What I could not have anticipated was that the room would be full of people who I would have never expected. This wasn't a milestone birthday or anything worth doing something extravagant, but for some reason my husband decided to go all out.

Later that night when all the festivities concluded and I was resting my head comfortably on the pillow that is cloud-nine euphoria, I rolled over and asked my husband why he'd made the day so special. His answer was simple: "Because you deserve it," he said softly while falling asleep.

As I replayed the day's events in my head, I was hit with the deep revelation that perhaps I truly did deserve this special treatment. Much like the mental barricade that hindered my ability to fully receive the love of God, I had to realize that my previous experiences with life and love had kept me from fully seeing my own worth. My husband's desire to celebrate my life was not based on criteria. There was no quota that determined whether I would be celebrated. His answer could have been because I did this or that, but it ended simply with "because you." In his eyes my existence commanded the type of celebration that was difficult for even me to receive.

I am reminded how God sees us in moments like that. We might believe that love should be based on conditions or behavior, but He decides to bless us because of who we are in His eyes. I had to make a conscious decision in the middle of my husband honoring me to *receive* the love that he was giving me. I think a part of me had been afraid that if I received his love, then I would come to need it or trust it. When you've spent a lifetime guarded and hoping to stay in control, placing yourself in a position where another person becomes a permanent fixture in your life is scary. But that's exactly what we must do if we're going to be in relationship with God.

I remember hearing the phrase "God-fearing" Christian. I thought that it meant we should be afraid of what will happen if we disappoint God. I am now coming to the realization that we should be in such close relationship with Him that we're afraid to do life without Him. The mere thought of making life decisions or destiny-altering choices without first praying and hearing from Him should be scary.

When you reach that place of complete trust in Him, you begin to live with expectation. As genuinely surprised as I was that my husband went out of his way to make my birthday special, there were these clues all along the way that let me know something was taking place. I could not fully quantify it nor did I know the details, but I knew that as distracted as I was with living in the moment, there was already something taking place in the future that was far better than what I could see.

That's how God is orchestrating our lives. He allows us to think things are going to go one way, but only so that He can get us properly positioned for what He has in mind. What overwhelmed me the most about what Touré did was less about how well he was able to secretly put everything together and more about how incredibly treasured I felt. I could not believe that he thought so much of me that he would allow me to believe my present joy of distractions would pale in comparison to what he was actually planning to do. Sometimes we can become so busy looking for reasons why we are loved that we fail to embrace the fact that we are loved.

My relationship with God has become less about me wondering *why* He loves me and more on enjoying the fact that He *does* love me. When you begin to truly expect and trust the love of God, it significantly changes your paradigm. I want you to live in a place of expectation. You must begin to expect that everything in your life, good or bad, has been divinely assigned to help God manifest the divine purpose and intentions He has for you.

When you've experienced disappointment in the past, living with that level of expectation can be scary. We convince ourselves that it's better to expect nothing at all than to expect something and be disappointed. This is where trusting God comes into play. You have to trust that even in your disappointment there is a bigger, better plan taking place behind the scenes that you cannot see. God has plans for your life so unfathomable that when you look back on how it all came together, you will know that it took divine resources to make it all work.

So where do you start?

Trusting God comes down to first making peace with your path. You can't resent where you are or what you've been through and expect the best. Bitterness and joy cannot dwell in the same home. As we read in James 1:8, "A double minded man is unstable in all his ways" (KJV). If you're going to truly embrace the love that is constantly surrounding you, you're going to have to become more honest and transparent in your life than you've ever been. God's power is made strong in our lives when it is met with the frailty of our human experience. He wants to show us that He has been with us through every moment we've ever faced, but

Bitterness and joy cannot dwell in the same home.

we'll have to ask Him to give us the vulnerability required to see His hand on our lives. Beneath our tough exteriors and the stories we've had to tell ourselves to survive is the truth that many of us have been functioning while broken. God already has a plan to restore all that we feel we've lost, but we must be willing to cry out to Him first.

I want to share a prayer with you that helped me through my own reconciliation with God.

> *God, I've been searching for You my entire life. I've been hoping that I would hear Your voice in my darkest days. I have to ask for forgiveness because honestly I gave up on the idea that You had a plan for me. I've been so hurt by life and disappointed by my own actions that I learned to live a life that kept You at a distance. I didn't want to come to trust You. I didn't want to come to need You. I didn't want to let You down. I've felt so unworthy of Your blessings, but also so envious of other people who seem to access them so easily. I'm ready to turn my life around and focus on You more diligently. Help me to look back on my life and see Your fingertips. Help me to see that even when I was in trouble You had a plan that allowed me to escape. I've been bruised and broken, but somehow I've still survived. I've been searching for a sign that You've heard my prayers, that You hear my cries, and that I matter to You. I see now that the only reason this book is in my hands is so I could receive the reminder*

I've been looking for. Please take away any part of my mind, heart, or soul that would threaten to rob me of the knowledge that You love me. Break any connections I have with negativity. Help me to protect the light You've placed inside of me so that I may shine again. My life has been so far from perfect. My journey has been so difficult, but I'm still here. I still believe that You have plans for me. Give me the patience to receive that revelation, the strength to live it, and the voice that declares Your love is not about perfection but about those willing to admit their brokenness so that You may fill them up. In Jesus' name.

Reciting a version of this prayer in your heart and allowing it to resonate in your actions will help manifest the destiny God has for your life. We live in a world that is full of so much darkness. You can hardly turn on the news without hearing about death or destruction. If we aren't careful, we will begin to believe more in darkness than we do in the power of light to drive that darkness away. Our affinity for little babies and children is because the purity of their light has not been diminished by painful life experiences. Somewhere along the way that light gets harder and harder to find, but it never disappears. Regardless of what happens to us in life, that flicker of light exists for as long as we have air in our lungs. That light is the breath of God inside of us that could not be killed or squandered. That light is what makes us search for materials that sharpen our spiritual walk. That light is what brings a smile to our lips when we think we have no reason to smile. That light is in the kindness of two strangers having an exchange. That light is the Spirit of God that is available to us. We access that Spirit when we choose to be love and light in a world full of darkness. Greater than the experiences that have desensitized you is the light that is shining inside of you. You are the light that my children need. It's not enough to admire the brightness of someone else's light if you aren't willing to do the work that increases the shine of your own light.

I pray that this book reminds you that in spite of what you've gone through you are still lighter than darkness. I need your light to survive. I need it to grow bright and strong. I need our lights to combine. Your connection to me is much greater than connecting through words. It's bigger than whether we have similar stories or polar opposite journeys. You are connected to the God in me. The God in me that I wasn't sure would survive through my detours. But I have been forced to make a decision over and over again to walk in the consciousness of expecting beautiful God things in spite of my mistakes. I've had to pray for the discipline to live a life that I can be proud God is watching over, but to not be afraid to ask for help when I need it. I'm far from perfect, but I am trying. That's more than I can say about my past. I'd completely given up, but I believe that the pursuit of my light created a passionate pursuit that led to this book being in your hands. Imagine where your light will take you when you begin to trust God and not the negative opinions or thoughts that live in your heart. Serve eviction notice on any- and everything that has kept you from embracing the beauty and determination of your spirit. The commitment to protecting your connection with God is what gives you the faith to walk on water.

8

Purpose

I want my life to represent something bigger than just another person occupying space on earth. I want to look back on my life and feel as though I've made the world a better place. This is more than just surviving until I get the next check. I want a life no one would have to pay me to show up for. When I look at this world full of terror and disgrace, I wonder if there is an idea or talent inside of me that could answer someone's prayer. I know that I do not have all of these scars for nothing. I have to believe they will serve a purpose much larger than what I can see now. My life will be a gift to this world. I just have to figure out how to unwrap the issues that keep me from seeing the gift of being me.

I had only been home one short month when my mother asked me if I could help her organize and structure the women's ministry of our church. My initial reaction was to propose a few candidates who were more likely to be equipped to manifest the vision she had for the ministry. At the time I only knew a handful of scriptures and I could not tell you quickly where any of those were located. I certainly had the administrative and organizational skills she was looking for, but the idea of ministry made me cringe. My mother is a pint-size bully with a heart of gold, so it only took a few pleading blinks of her eyes before I was caving in to the pressure of helping her out.

I was sure to tell the women upfront that I was not campaigning to be their pastor or ministry leader. I was simply helping my mother until someone better came along. The restructuring that I oversaw was mostly structural at first. I utilized my previous experience working with the government to create processes and structures that would alleviate some of the recurring communication issues we were experiencing. With the support of an incredible internal team and hundreds of volunteers, we focused on revamping each program we offered to fit the needs of the women in our pews. It didn't take long before I was offering suggestions on program sessions and topics that would have been helpful to me presently or at another time in my life.

The fresh speakers and topics that we were covering intrigued everyone from staff to the ladies attending our events. Initially I was simply glad to help my mother, but when women started stopping me and thanking me, I knew I was in trouble. How could I ever stop helping God expose these women to the depths of their perseverance and strength? I'd always vowed that I would never *ever* be in ministry. It was the one thing I thought I knew for sure about my life.

In hindsight, I wonder if I'd made that promise because I simply wasn't sure that my life was suitable for a life of ministry. Nevertheless, one constant seemed undeniable and that was that women were coming into the knowledge of their creativity and limitless possibilities because of what I was able to do within that ministry. I was beginning to feel the fulfillment of a life that was bigger than me. There were rewards that money could not quantify, and I found satisfaction in watching another woman find her wings. It then dawned on me why the ministry had so many faithful volunteers. The volunteer staff was not serving to be seen. They were helping because the women on the other end of their service were a reflection of who they were or have been before.

You do not choose purpose. Purpose chooses you. When something on the inside of you connects with what's happening outside of you, it is a sign that a portion of your life is a part of the solution. The first step to fulfilling your purpose is allowing yourself to have one. We can get caught up with a list of things we are never going to do, but then become dissatisfied with the life that we possess. If you're going to tap in to the unlimited potential that is available to you, then you must remove the limits from your life. I am even willing to venture out on a limb and suggest that if you have a strong aversion to something, but constantly have the opportunity to do it, your purpose may be tracking you down.

When something on the inside of you connects with what's happening outside of you, it is a sign that a portion of your life is a part of the solution.

So, let's qualify this idea of purpose. The first thing to understand about purpose is that it will always be rooted in service toward the betterment of humanity. If you're looking for work or service that catapults you into riches and fame, then you should skip this chapter because that's not what purpose is about at all. Your purpose is the answer to a problem that plagues our world.

That purpose can be manifest in a variety of different fields and ways, but you cannot determine whether it is purpose until you can qualify why you're doing whatever it is that you do.

If you ask me why I have dedicated my life and platforms to the empowerment of individuals who have struggled with insecurities, my answer would be simple. I want to encourage people to look beyond their flaws and issues and dare to fall in love with their imperfection. I want my life to serve as evidence that genuine encounters with God produce radical change in your life. I now realize that when I began helping in the women's ministry—even against my better judgment—I was having a radical encounter with the unfolding of my purpose.

Quite honestly, I believe my aversion to helping in the women's ministry was based on fear of how I would be received. I did not want to come off as one of those weird religious Christians who are constantly making other people uncomfortable. Though I had a genuine relationship with God, I felt that it was different from what would be considered normal in sphere of influence, and I was right! The thing that I thought would isolate me from connecting with the women was ultimately the very thing that made me stand out among them. What came naturally to me then was an extraordinary blessing to others.

Your purpose is not going to wake you up one day, flail its arms, and say, "Hey! I'm your purpose; let's go make the world a better place." You may have already identified your purpose, but it came so easily to you that you did not realize it was a gift. Your talent does not give you purpose; it is how you apply your talent that does. How many times have we seen entertainers who were extremely gifted but tormented? When the applause fades and life fails to give you the feeling of substance, you begin to feel empty.

Once you begin to uncover the talents and gifts of your life, your first goal should not be learning how to "cash in" on them. The question you must ask yourself is, *How do I use this gift to make the world a better place to live in for years to come?*

Avoid the misconception that purpose is limited to a select few. Every person on earth has a reason for being here. Our mission is to show ourselves worthy of and responsible for carrying the burden of that purpose.

Your purpose is not a democracy that requires the votes and validation of your circle. So many people fail to discover their purpose when they make it about the appearance they desire their lives to have. You cannot have an image in your head of what you want your life to look like and ask God to mold

You must be willing to let go of the dream you have for your life so that He can give you His plans.

you how He sees fit. Those are conflicting requests that will ultimately create a war within you. The beauty of the free will given to us by God is both loving and dangerous. It's dangerous because guidance from Him requires humility. You must be willing to let go of the dream you have for your life so that He can give you His plans. When we sacrifice our lives on the altar of God's plan, He give us much more than we could ever ask for.

Only You Can Determine Your Purpose

My legit dream in life was to be someone's wife. I thought that because of my love for cooking and creating a warm environment at home my purpose would center around domestication. These thoughts were constantly validated by the thoughts and opinions of family members. Trusting their vantage point of my life, I began to create a dream that fit the most obvious choice for my life. It took me some time to learn that simply being good at something does not mean it should be your purpose. In fact, it is the mystery of your potential that makes it clear God's thoughts are higher than ours. If the people around you could determine what your future is supposed to look like, you would have no need to ask God to direct your path. No one knows but Him what you were placed on this earth to do, but there are some foundational tools that can assist you in beginning to see and constantly maintain His plan for you.

One of the first pieces of advice that I want to offer to you is this: don't trust the sign you're looking for; trust the one you never expected to see. Have you ever prayed one of those prayers that you knew could not fail? For example, "God, if You want me to call my ex-boyfriend back, then let my phone turn on when I press the power button." It's highly unlikely that your full cell phone battery would suddenly become empty, but these are the kind of prayers we recite when we're determined to find a way to get our way. I'll never forget the time I was sitting in my closet in my Texas home daydreaming. To be honest, I wasn't quite daydreaming as much as I was focusing intently on all of the reasons I should break up with my boyfriend, now husband. *He loves you too much,* I thought to myself. *You're bound to disappoint him sooner or later, so you might as well get it over with now.* The thoughts were running a marathon in my mind. *He's probably only with you because he's a pastor and he really wants access to your father.* Insecurity after insecurity formed in my mind trying to convince me to relinquish the idea of genuine love being available to me.

Right in the middle of my slightly schizophrenic mental dialogue, Touré called me. Since I was distracted by my thoughts, I didn't mind that he was replying to e-mails while we were on the phone. Just as the last thought about him plotting a romance with me to get closer to my father was fully crystalizing in my mind, he began to proofread his biography in an e-mail he received. Speaking aloud, he began to correct the author's summary of his life by adding in the accomplishments, hard work, and determination that had allowed for our paths to cross in the first place. The editing of the e-mail made one thing very clear, quite frankly: He was not with me because he needed my last name. He was there because he was trying to replace it with his. I wasn't looking for that sign, but like a stick hitting me over the head, it was there. That moment, and countless others like them, became the signs that confirmed what I was feeling regarding Touré's role in my life. God sent him to love me on purpose! Not only would our connection deepen the roots of my personal relationship with God, it also taught me so much about myself.

What Purpose Requires

I have learned that it's not enough to have raw talent or chemistry if you are not willing to do the work to take it from good to better. In order to be effective, purpose requires discipline. What separates talented people from purposeful ones is what they're willing to face to become better in their craft. I want to share with you the disciplines you must master to manifest a long-standing purpose.

The first one is the discipline of commitment. In this fast-paced, instant-gratification society, staying in one field takes patience few possess. When you become too consumed with the notion that life is passing you by, you miss pivotal training necessary to giving your purpose lasting power. We are often motivated to accelerate our progress because we see other people excelling seemingly quicker than us. The anxious feeling of being left behind forces us to make erratic decisions that only further confuse our lives. The hard pill that very few want to swallow is that if you were ready to be catapulted to the heights that you admire, then opportunities would have presented themselves that led you there. You can't allow the success of others or fear of failure to force you to make unwise decisions regarding your future. I may be a little too late with this nugget for some of you, but guess what? It's still not too late to allow God to set the pace for your life.

Regardless of how off track your life may seem, you are exactly where you need to be. This is the training ground that will prepare you in some capacity for what is next in your life. I was once a receptionist. I dropped out of college and needed to find steady income quickly. Fast-forward to my life now, and though I no longer sit at a desk answering phones, I do work closely with our Los Angeles–based team. I'm able to help train and mentor receptionists on how to handle guests, maintain office environments, set up for meetings, and handle demanding callers. The position you're in now may be the one you are selected to hire for later. If you fail to fully apply yourself and understand the intricacies of that position, you won't know what to look for later. You have to begin to ask yourself, "How can I challenge myself to max out my potential on this level?" When you make up your mind to find innovative ways to streamline your functionality, you prove to those watching around you and God above you that you'll work just as hard on the next level as you are on the current level. Do you have the discipline to not just stay, but to stay and execute with excellence and reliability?

The next discipline that purpose requires is focus. Have you ever been to one of those sports bars where there are multiple televisions playing different things at one time? I have found myself so intrigued by all of them that it's difficult to just watch one at a time! That was until the Dallas Cowboys began playing like they wanted to head to the Super Bowl a couple of years ago. Every Sunday after service we would stop by a local restaurant that would allow us to catch the remaining few minutes of the game. It didn't matter what was playing on the other television screens surrounding the one with my beloved Dallas Cowboys. I was intensely focused; the outcome mattered to me.

When God's destiny for your life begins to outweigh the distractions around you, you're honing the gift of focus. Since I am a football fan in general, it would have been easy to glance from screen to screen while half-watching the Cowboys. But I knew that at any moment one play could change the entire game, and I wanted to witness the momentum when that occurred.

One phone call, one e-mail, one comment, one moment could change the momentum of your life. If you're too busy trying to appease the distractions in your life, you may miss the opportunity that was meant to reveal something exceptional about yourself.

You want another reason why you need to have the discipline to focus? Not only because excelling in your purpose depends on it, but also because how excellently you produce your purpose does as well. Too often we can become so consumed with excelling and going to the next level that we don't take the time to perfect our gift on the level that we're on. Here's the reality: many people have the gift you currently possess, but what they do not have is your heart and unique ability to translate that gift into the world and culture. That's why you can't be saddened when you see people who appear to be taking over in a certain arena. Just because someone is doing well does not mean your gift has become null and void. You must be willing to not be distracted by someone else's progress long enough to see your growth.

I can remember when I first began public speaking I was so nervous! I intentionally requested a handheld microphone because my hands shook. I figured that if I was holding the microphone then I would be able to stabilize my hands. My voice would rise from its normal octave to a high-pitched screech when the nerves took over. I wish I could tell you that the more I spoke the less those things happened, but I would be lying. Instead, I learned that my nerves were distracting me from my mission and ultimately deterring me from my purpose.

Your inner emotions and insecurities play a greater role in distracting you from bringing forth the gifts that are inside of you more than the external ones you have. God has given you the divine strategy and capability to control your life. You don't have to wait for people to understand you before you begin to develop. The reality is that people understand you by what they observe of you. If you're a people pleaser seeking validation, then people will understand that they'll always be able to get you to abandon your mission and give them your focus. Prioritize your life! Anyone who penalizes you for pursuing inner excellence will punish you when you acquire external success. If they cannot handle your hustle, they won't be able to celebrate your victories. Don't be discouraged when people fail to understand why your focus on what matters the most is increasing.

Having the discipline to focus on purpose when nothing else is distracting you is easy. It's when you have pleasant distractions that things become more challenging. There are times when life requires balance to make sure all areas of your life are being attended to. The only thing with those moments is that you have to determine what to place on hold while you focus on something else. Sometimes we can become so consumed with tending to our world that we neglect the very things that give us a personal sense of fulfillment and purpose.

You will have to protect your purpose from the things in life that are often the source of your joy but don't necessarily challenge you to move forward. Otherwise you will sacrifice long-term progress for temporary gratification. You will come to a place where you trust that anyone who can't handle hearing no from you should not have the power to control you. I think we're often afraid to say no because we fear how it will affect the other person, but we don't consider how saying yes can harm us. Of course there are times as wives, mothers, sisters, and friends when we sacrifice or rearrange our lives, but those relationships offer us unparalleled reciprocity. Relationships that grow us into more patient, kind, Christlike people will not be easy. They will certainly require sacrifice, but we never sacrifice more than what God is willing to give us in return. I really want us to focus on the relationships that require a sacrifice of our goals, mission, and God-ordained destiny. If you can't handle my no, it's because you are too comfortable abusing my yes.

The third discipline you must learn in the pursuit of purpose is learning to lose. Yes, this is the part few people want to hear. The truth is, no matter how incredible you are or how ready you feel, you are going to take some *L*s along the road to purpose.

Those losses are so devastating that they convince many to give up. Wins are only sweet because losses have been so bitter. If you want to see your life fully maximized, you will have to learn some lessons that only come from losing. Losing teaches you how to maneuver for the next time. It allows you to recognize your own weaknesses. Losing can give you an edge that winning does not afford you. Losing makes you desperate to get better, do more, and work harder. Every loss carries with it an opportunity for you to examine your actions and thoughts to make sure they are perfectly aligned with what God has for you.

There will be some opportunities you lose so that you can be forced into something better. God never takes away anything from us that He doesn't return with interest! I told you about the story of Ruth being one of my favorite ones in the Bible. Did I tell you about how she lost her first husband? Her first husband's family fled to her homeland because there was a famine in their nation. Before they could reestablish themselves in their new home or plan to return to their native country, all of the men in his family died. Unfortunately, this included Ruth's husband.

God never takes away anything from us that He doesn't return with interest!

As if his death wasn't traumatic enough for Ruth to deal with, she had the added factor of being alienated by the people in her hometown. You see, Ruth had to convert religions in order to marry her first husband. I can imagine how her emotions must have played with her. She went out on a limb to marry a man much different from her. She gave up everything she knew to be joined with him and then that dream died.

Committed to keeping her promise to her mother-in-law,

she returned to her deceased husband's hometown. Desperate to survive by any means necessary, she began gleaning grain in the fields. At that time hardly anyone knew her, so she dallied behind the groups. She had no way of knowing that her positioning would ultimately lead to her being noticed by the owner of the field. Through a series of events she went from working in his fields to being the object of his affection. Then she went from being the object of his affection to his wife. If it were not for the loss of her husband, she would not have been redeemed by a man who went above and beyond to care for her.

I am in no way suggesting that what Ruth and her first husband possessed was not special. It was actually a necessary loss that she had to endure in order to learn about the existence and culture of Boaz, the owner of the fields and eventual father to her firstborn son. What may look like a loss to you is actually an opportunity for God. If Ruth's original plan had worked out, she would have been married to a man afraid of famine, but God had predestined for her to build a life with a man who had abundance. God's plans are always bigger and better than our own. So don't be discouraged when plans fall apart. God will use those very same pieces to build something new.

Though there are countless other disciplines that could be added to this chapter, the last one I want to tell you about is the one that is very near to my heart. That is the discipline to learn. Sometimes we don't like to admit that we don't know certain things because we're afraid that it will make us look dumb or unworthy of being in certain positions. Don't allow your ego to bar you from the education you need to understand the circle God has placed you in.

Growing up, I remember my father quoting Proverbs 18:16 in his sermons: "A man's gift makes room for him, and brings him before great men." Many would become excited because they translated this to mean that their gift would make them like the "great men" in their presence. I want to challenge this notion to look deeper at the idea of someone being "before" great men. True enough, the greatness is a reflection of what's inside of us, but that does not always mean that greatness has been cultivated. When you are in a room of people smarter or more accomplished than you, don't fall into the trap of trying to prove you deserve to be in there by verbose speaking. Don't let your mouth overcompensate for your insecurities. The best thing you can do when in a room of great people is study what makes them great.

Your gift may get you in the room, but your wisdom and strategy are what will keep you in it. If you are too proud to admit that you don't know something, then all you'll ever have is what you currently know. The philosopher Socrates said, "The only thing that I know is that I know nothing." Learning is a sign of humility, not weakness. Having the hunger to search for information that will sharpen your craft fuels your ability to help not only yourself but others. Let go of the idea that you've "arrived" in life. There's no such thing. Even the Bible reminds us that the work God is doing in our lives is constant.

I've learned many things from watching my parents' lives change over the years. One of the things I'm most proud of is how I've seen my father break down barriers in so many different arenas. From music, television, film, and ministry he realized that his potential did not have to be limited to what people were accustomed to seeing. If God calls you to help the homeless, it can begin with making sandwiches in your kitchen, but it can ultimately transform into renovating buildings and providing temporary housing, or creating programs that teach them skills to navigate the workplace. That transition will expand the reach of people you're able to help, but it may also call you to understand how to navigate the construction process, business development, and grant funding. You can't let what you don't know intimidate you from learning more. Only foolish people don't believe they have areas to grow.

The desire to increase your discipline in these areas for the manifestation of your purpose can only be fueled by one thing: passion. If you have to place pictures on your wall of the people you're meant to help, do it! If you need a daily reminder of the goals you must pursue, then write them down. Do whatever it takes to discover, refine, and release what God has placed inside of you.

9

Intimacy

I want to be seen, but I'm afraid you won't like what you see. I've taken quite a few lickings, but my heart is still ticking. I wish that I could offer you an unscathed heart that has never been damaged. I want to give you the best of me and tuck the broken parts away in a place you'll never discover. But I know far too well the pain that is caused when a love is built on a lie. So I won't protect you from my truth, I won't pretend that things haven't happened to me. I will wear my life proudly because it made me who I am. I will not allow the fear of rejection to convince me to make our relationship a stage. I want to be the person you always dreamed of doing life with, but I must know, did your vision make a provision for an imperfect person with a soul made of gold? If I show you the scars that created my smile, could you still hold my hand? If I said my prayers within the range of your ears, would you turn and walk away or will we join hands and summon angels? I don't want to know your favorite color as much as I want to know what motivates you to fight away negativity. I'm not looking for company, I'm searching for a warrior whose forces I can join with mine to build a *bigger, brighter future. I want to show you who I am and how I became, but I'm going to need time to trust your eyes can handle what's behind mine.*

There's going to come a time on this journey when you have an encounter with another soul that intrigues you with such intensity that you begin to toy with the idea of having genuine intimacy.

Unfortunately the word *intimacy* has become synonymous with sex, and what I'm talking about is much deeper than the physical act of two people coming together. True intimacy is when two souls begin to intertwine in such a way that you can no longer tell where one person's soul begins and where the other's ends. It is the most exhilarating feeling in the world, but I can tell you from experience that it is also terrifying. It awakens insecurities within you that you thought you mastered or perhaps didn't even know existed. Suddenly, you are consumed with the realization that someone is going to be viewing the entirety of your life with intense evaluation. Above all else you hope that they'll decide, as you have, that your love is more valuable because of what you've experienced, not less. Still, you can't help but fear that they will reject you and go running in the opposite direction. I can remember the thoughts that raced through my head when I realized that I was going to have to open myself up to my husband in a way that I wasn't honestly sure I could handle. True love is far from comfortable; it's more challenging than the superficial connections that often fill our voids. That's why it's difficult to find and maintain. It demands authenticity, vulnerability, and trust.

Before that moment comes, there are some things that you must work out regarding your previous relationships. Disappointments in relationships affect you. Just because you have the justification to leave a relationship does not mean that the relationship did not create and establish an unhealthy paradigm for you. I recognized this for myself on a drive to a business meeting with my husband.

"I will never cheat on you," Touré said while we drove through the Hollywood canyons. I grew silent and nodded my head. The conversation shifted to another subject quickly. I was relieved. There were a few times after that when he pledged his fidelity that warranted a similar, silent response from me. I wasn't really sure what I was supposed to say. "Thank you?" The subject made me totally uncomfortable. From the time we met, Touré had been this euphoric fantasy of love that I flirted with giving up on. I didn't even want to entertain the thought that he could possibly cheat on me, so his promising that he would not do so forced me to consider that possibility. Or at least that's what I told him when he finally asked why I seemed to become uncomfortable whenever he brought it up. I wasn't sure why at the time; I just knew that I didn't like the way I felt when he promised to be faithful.

"I think you either think I'm going to cheat on you one day or feel you may cheat on me," Touré said the next time my discomfort was obvious during the conversation. I was caught off guard by his statement, but I could not even properly defend myself. I wanted to offer him a series of shocked expressions that would assure him the mere thought of it was too much to fathom. The truth was, however, that I had been exposed to the most unreliable aspects of human behavior (my own included) and I'd determined not to put too much weight on words or promises. I preferred to live my life hoping for the best and pretending the worst did not exist.

That was a mistake that I want to help you avoid.

Do people mess up in relationships? Absolutely! Will you be perfect when you enter one? Absolutely not! Does that mean you should modify your expectations to the level of a person's insecurities? Heck to the naw!

You are going to have to come to terms with the fact that your experiences may have persuaded you to change your expectations for love, relationships, or marriage to accommodate a margin of human failure that could occur. Many of us make a decision to prepare for the worst and avoid expecting the best. We foolishly believe that the best way to safeguard our hearts is to avoid setting high expectations. You cannot avoid disappointment by becoming comfortable with low expectations. I can't tell you how many times I've heard conversations among women I admire suggesting that since all men cheat they have a standard for them to adhere to. In other words, they would prefer to have a man who has a level of discretion when he cheats. I've overheard various conversations that suggest that men who cheat must keep protecting their partner in mind. The philosophy of "as long as you don't bring it into my home, and make sure you keep it out of my face" has set a precedent for relationships that I'd become comfortable with. It was not until my husband challenged my silence on fidelity that I had to confront my thought process.

Boys Versus Men

If you find yourself repeatedly falling for boys pretending to be men, you must ask yourself what the little girl inside of you is crying out for and hoping to receive from them. Relationships that we choose reflect the relationship we have with ourselves. If you're constantly disappointed with the dynamics of your romantic life, then you are replicating a disappointment you experienced that changed your ability to expect and receive pure love. You must be willing to ask yourself when and why you changed. My unwillingness to receive the commitment of loyalty and faithfulness from the man I'd married was not just because I didn't want to consider it. It was because a part of me was unsure that that kind of promise could be kept. It dawned on me that fidelity, like most of the character traits people value, is intentional. It's a decision that someone makes because of who they are and what they feel about the person they're with. People who have been hurt cheat other people out of the sense of security that stabilizes a relationship.

My imperfect husband was creating a goal for himself in our marriage and I was requesting that he lower the bar or not mention it at all. I wanted to make the same vow, but I was afraid that I would be incapable of keeping it. There were countless things I said I would never do that I ended up doing anyway. Incidentally, I was not sure that I could trust myself to be the type of person I wanted to give my love to. It would have been so easy for me to justify my inability to fully say those words in return based on how imperfect people are, but I believe that I received a revelation that altered my perspective on intimate relationships.

Humanity certainly plays a role in relationships, but we have access to a higher power. That role does not have to be stronger than the strength of our divinity. A person being human is not a license for them to anticipate the possibilities of hurt being a not-too-distant reality. You should have a love that causes you to increase your character and overcome your fears. There's a scripture in 1 John that says, "Perfect love casts out fear" (4:18 ESV).

The only way our love reaches perfection is through handing our hearts over to God and asking Him to show us our fears. Don't give another person permission to hold your heart unless you know their hands belong to God.

When your partner's heart and hands belong to God, they won't just hold your heart; they will also cast out the fears that have made their home in your heart. Loving someone with all of your heart is a popular quote, but very few people actually achieve this level of intimacy. Loving someone with all of your heart means trusting them with your brokenness too. It requires that you trust them with your dreams and mistakes, your vulnerabilities and strengths, your smiles and tears. True love produces worship—not of the other person, but of God for bringing that person into your life. This is not about finding a hero who will save you from all of the failed relationships of your past. This is about finding your strength to soar and having an encounter with another soul determined to feel the wind blowing in their face as they climb to new heights. This experience will be like nothing you've ever felt before and everything you've ever needed to have in your life.

True love produces worship—not of the other person, but of God for bringing that person into your life.

My husband and I tend to stick with our favorite places to eat. When we find a good spot, we avoid venturing out too much, but we made a vow to begin exploring some of the local places in our neighborhood. After dining at an incredible sushi spot in our neighborhood, we walked around the busy shopping center holding hands and enjoying the California sun. I had to admit even I couldn't believe how picturesque my life had become. I jokingly tell my husband all the time that if I were on the outside looking in on our relationship, I would be grossed out and slightly annoyed by our constant affection. Still, as we strolled hand in hand I couldn't help but feel as though I were floating on a cloud.

That euphoric feeling was interrupted when our stop at the local gelato shop turned into a competitive game of checkers. I love the game of checkers. It's been one of my favorite games since childhood. I was the reigning champ in my family. I'd been enjoying my retirement as the undefeated champion when my husband challenged me to a game. I was torn. Would I allow this moment of romantic tranquility, peace, and civility to be jeopardized by the victory I was sure to clench? My competitive husband began setting up the board before I could make my decision. Soon we were three games in and I was being demolished. The trash talk was at an all-time high, and we were far from looking like the two lovebirds who had been strolling hand in hand only moments ago. It made no sense to me. I started the game the way I always had when I was a kid. It was a sure thing each time regardless of who I played with except for him. I was baffled. That quickly turned to slight irritation as he transitioned from victory to coaching me. As if three losses were grounds for some intervention from the competition!

My ego was so bruised that we decided to let the last game end in a draw. After a few weeks passed we sat down to play checkers again. He made one statement before beginning that explained to me his objective when starting a game. In that moment I realized that we had two totally different intentions when playing the game. My goal was to play the way I've always played, but his was to study the moves I make and create his strategy from there. It was in that moment that I realized what has made our intimate relationship different from anything I've ever experienced in the past. I started most of my relationships the same way. I would balance the attention I gave a suitor, showing him semi-interest, but not so much that it might come off as aggressive. I was careful not to say certain things and to always be guarded.

My encounter with Touré was much different because I was not living by a set of "dating game rules." I was armed with the wisdom of my experiences and a clear vision and standard for the kind of people I wanted to be in my life. Much like that game of checkers, I learned through him that the relationships that truly make a difference in our lives are the ones that require us to break out of our patterns and rhythms. They force us to examine our intentions, motives, and ways. They make us realize that if we do things the way we've always done them, we'll get the results we've always had. If you want to constantly win at this thing called love, you have to be willing to let go of every misconception you've ever had about relationships and roles.

Heart Posture

There is no perfect formula for finding your mate, but there is a heart posture that allows you to see and choose wisely whom God has for you. God does not operate on the timing of our biological clocks, nor does He use our insecurities as motivation to rush us into relationships. When we learn to be content with His plan and His timing for our lives, we are given the beautiful gift of falling deeper in love with Him, ourselves, and the life He's given us. You don't have to rush what God has ordained.

I hope you marry the person God placed on this earth for

you. I hope you choose to believe that love is not an illusion, but a tangible gift that makes life sweeter. I pray your previous experiences, or lack thereof, do not convince you that your heart wasn't made to love. I pray the person God has for you makes every heartbreak worth it. I hope you see the beauty in starting over and over again with the same person. If you don't silence your heart after it's been hurt, there will come a point on your journey when you admit that in spite of what you've gone through, you want an encounter with someone who makes you wonder if you're ready for love. If your moment is anything like mine, it will be magical. It will create a longing within you that you didn't even realize existed, but if you take a moment to reflect, you'll see the signs were there. It was in the way you settled. It was in the way you gave so much when the other person returned so little.

I have a hard truth to share with you regarding those moments. It may be challenging initially, but recognize that I can only speak to it because I've been there. If I could have shared a message with the broken girl searching for love that I once was, I would tell her this.

You can no longer afford to trust the treasure that is your heart to anyone who says you're beautiful. Anyone can admire a diamond, but few recognize the quality and care required to keep it beautiful. For too long your insecurities made you so desperate for attention that you handed over your golden heart to people who've only handled glitter. This is not their fault; it's yours. You ignored the signs, hoping they would wake up one day and see your worth. The truth is it's time for you to wake up. You can no longer go through life unconsciously hurting yourself and asking someone else to heal you. The power for you to overcome is already inside of you. The longer you stay, the more you deny the strength you have to move on. You're better than the hurt you've subscribed to. There is still beauty inside of you. There's nothing you've lost in this process that can't be restored, but you must determine how you will spend your grace. Don't give your patience away to people who will abuse it. Don't give your courage away to people who don't understand it. Surround yourself with people who can reciprocate what you pour. Let their validation be an overflow that allows you to touch the lives of other broken people. This is bigger than you. This is about redefining love and esteem in a culture determined to make us feel less than. You are the hero you've been looking for. So put on your cape, get off of your knees, and stop begging for someone to love you. Love yourself. Seek God and all other things will be added to you.

Making the decision to share your life with someone is a major decision. Pursuing a lifetime of intimacy and trust sounds like a fairy tale, but the truth is it takes more work than people fully realize. I never fully understood marriage until I met Touré. Whenever I heard couples saying they had been married for sixty years, I would wonder to myself, *Why would anyone do that? You could have three long successful marriages in that time.* Yes, you can judge me. The truth is that I was basing that thought on my experience with marriage. Devotion in a marriage that does not require authentic intimacy makes it optional for the people involved. In previous relationships I never fully gave my heart away, only my hopes and dreams. Hopes and dreams are intangible desires, but the current state of your tender heart can only be given to someone you trust. Since I never experienced that level of trust, I could not relate to relationships that did. Reciprocity in relationships provides for deeper levels of understanding and intimacy.

Gratitude

I can remember when my daughter Makenzie became old enough to really appreciate gifts. If parents are honest, they'll tell you the first few birthdays and Christmases are great for memory books, but the child hardly knows what's going on. There comes a time, however, when they're old enough to show gratitude for the items you've worked to provide for them. For Makenzie it was her fourth birthday. "This is the *best* day of my life!" she exclaimed as she opened the large box that held her toy car. She was in full mermaid regalia surrounded by a slew of her friends. She was on top of the world! Her reaction in that moment made up for the hours I spent the night before putting the car together.

Whether we choose to admit it, when we give to others, their reciprocity to us is not in what we receive materialistically; it's in their reaction. The reaction is what determines whether the investment was valued. The reaction is what determines whether you'll invest again. The same rule applies in relationships. Almost everything is about reaction. What do you get in return for your love? Loyalty? Trust? Commitment? Security? Think about the ultimate example of love. The Bible teaches us that God so loved the world that He gave [an action] His only Son so that whosoever believed [reaction] in Him would not perish, but have everlasting life. God didn't just give His only Son so that we could nod our heads and say, "Oh! That was nice." He gave His Son so that we could be so motivated by the depths of His love that we embarked on living a life that did not cave to fear.

The evidence that we were created in the image of God lies in our expectation for relationship. We're almost always willing to give of ourselves, but whether we admit it, it's in hopes of receiving a reaction that affirms our sacrifice. Eventually disappointment turns to heartbreak if we recognize that we may never receive the reaction we hoped for.

I know all too well how this goes.

The first time I got married I wasn't old enough to legally drink. That's not to knock people who marry young, but it is my personal admission that I married before I was mature or emotionally healthy enough to make a wise decision. I dropped out of college and finally found a steady job. Life was admittedly not going the way I expected. It seemed like my "prime time" to make something of my life had passed. I decided it was time to create as much stability as possible. I implemented a plan that seemed to mirror success for other people. I don't think I was a full thirty days into the marriage when it became clear that I had no idea what I was doing or why I signed up to do it.

You should never enter into a relationship with someone you would not want to become. That seems like such a simple rule, but you would be surprised how many people enter into relationships hoping their good deeds and fine looks will inspire change. They are met constantly with disappointment when their investment returns nothing to them. In the back of their minds, they begin to wonder if the lack of motivation their partners have to change is a direct reflection of their worth.

There's no way to qualify whether you're ready for a relationship until you've taken the time to fully understand your previous relationships. It's so easy to point the finger and place blame, but every failed relationship has at least two sets of fingerprints on it. You may have been victimized repeatedly, but in order to avoid repeating those cycles in your life you have to ask the tough questions. What was it about me that failed to heed the signs that were so obvious? Why did I become so desperate for love that I lost my power?

I meet so many women who choose to count love out because they've experienced one too many cheaters. Rarely have they taken the time to search within their souls to determine what role their insecurities may have played in attracting the same type of men repeatedly.

Once you're able to fully evaluate your own patterns and dysfunction, you must be willing to recognize what issues may exist in the person you're committing to, because regardless of how perfect someone seems, they, too, are evolving and working through challenges. There will come a time in every relationship when it becomes clear that you're not in a relationship with an idea; you're connected to a person. You'll have to resist the urge of measuring your relationship up to the ninety-minute romantic comedy we've all come to see as the ideal.

You're signing up to help someone sort through their issues, applaud their victories, and pray over their hurts. You won't always get it right, but the moments you do will help you survive the moments you don't. Whether you're married or single, I suggest you create a variation of this prayer to prepare your heart for the journey that is creating a lifelong connection with your spouse.

God, please soften my heart toward the person You've
predestined me to spend the rest of my life with. Help me to

*see them the way you see them, not through the eyes of my
selfish desires. Make me sensitive to the words they speak
and compassionate toward the ones too difficult for them to
say. Open my heart so that I can receive their love. Open
my mind so that I can understand how they became the
way they are. You have given me divine insight to help this
person fulfill their destiny on earth. Help me to not abuse
that power. Season my words with grace and douse my anger
with the knowledge that You've given me their heart to hold
because I'm capable of bringing out the best in it. Help me
to release them from the roles I needed them to play so that
I can see the strength in what they offer. Help me to release
disappointment and bitterness so that our home can be full
of Your presence. May Your Spirit saturate every part of our
relationship. May our union be worship to You. May our love
be a reminder that all things work together for good when
we answer the call to love like You do. Touch the heart of my
partner so that they, too, can see my vulnerability the way
that You do. Help me to stand before them with a naked soul,
but no shame. In Jesus' name.*

Are you truly prepared for the love you've prayed for? Are
you truly ready to be a partner? There's no way you can fully recognize the extent of that promise until you're smack dab in the
middle of fulfilling your word. *This is tough,* I thought to myself.
*How do I balance my needs and desires with the needs and desires of
the person to whom I've devoted my love?* Everyone wants love, but
no one wants the vulnerability love requires. One of the scari-
est parts about creating a life together is that you must succumb
to the fact that the existence of your ecosystem is not your sole

responsibility. Love is giving your power away and praying the other person won't abuse it, but being prepared to forgive if/when they do. Love requires sacrifice.

Love Like My Mother

This realization became crystal clear to me when Touré and I were six weeks post-partum from having our youngest daughter, Ella, and I'd basically kidnapped my mother from her responsibilities in Dallas. She placed her life on pause to tend to me in my time of need. She was in my kitchen cooking and humming the words to her favorite hymn when I sat down to help my daughter with her homework. I must admit it was so surreal to see my mother piddling around the same kitchen where I make the meals for my family now. I saw my mannerisms mirrored in her actions, and I smiled at the thought that with every day I am becoming more like her. My daughter will undoubtedly inherit many of our traits. Even in the early stages of her life, I saw pieces of me gifted from my mother present in Makenzie.

So much of our identity is defined by who we observe. Without much intentionality at all, I mimic the thoughts, expressions, and speech patterns of my mother. The more I evolve in my own essence, the more I am like her.

My thoughts began drifting to the connections I've made with people in the past. There came definitive breaking moments in our relationships when I could no longer continue to progress with them. Contrary to popular belief, not every disconnection has to end sourly, but it does become necessary for them to end. As I reflected on those moments in my life, I recognized one constant theme. I became frustrated when asking people to invest on a level they were literally incapable of understanding. I learned that having something in common does not equate to having the same character. Millions of people can listen to similar types of music or enjoy the same types of movies, but few are able to maintain the character necessary to stay in relationship with you.

This fact used to bring me hurt and even anger, but as I sat watching my mother and seeing myself, I realized that people cannot give you what they've never received. Hearing a challenging story about someone's family life or difficult past sends any compassionate person in search of a cape to save their day. This desire to rescue is a recipe for disaster. It doesn't take long before frustration kicks in and we begin to wonder why our best efforts aren't enough to bring about change. It's unrealistic to expect a person to change a lifetime habit after only knowing you for a few months or years. It's even more unrealistic to expect someone who never witnessed honor, integrity, wisdom, loyalty, or truth in their homes to offer it to you.

Certainly not every case is the same, and there are exceptions to every rule. By and large, though, most people are products of their environment. When people who've only experienced broken trust and heartbreak encounter the foreign object of love and loyalty, they may not respond the way you think they should. Your love may scare them before it can ever heal them. Your heart may break before it ever receives the trust you're searching for. It does not make them bad people or you a failure. It simply means that all they can offer in your life is what they've seen. Without their conscious and uncoerced decision to become better than what they've seen or experienced, their actions are bound to reflect the pain that lives in their hearts.

Here comes the difficult part. You'll have to become content with loving them if they never change or be brave enough to change yourself. Recognize that lasting change can only come from within; you will have to learn to stand by and pray that a radical encounter with God allows for transformation. Your faith may not yield the instant results you wish, but it's important that you stay committed for one reason and one alone: you love who they are, not who they have the potential to become. And if you leave, it will be for another reason altogether: you love who you are and are committed to seeing who you have the potential to become regardless of what you have to release in the process. At the end of the day, it's not about them or their process; it's about you.

Life may have dealt them a hand they're still trying to figure out, but it's dealing you one also. Just because you know better doesn't mean you always do better, and just because you do better doesn't always mean you know what lies ahead. One thing is for certain—as your evolution into the truest form of yourself takes place, you'll look back on moments, relationships, and connections like these and recognize that with each heartbreak you learned something new about yourself. Every shattered piece held a mystery that your future requires. Don't resent the time you spent trying to change someone else; just search for the ways that time changed you. The greatest gift you can give yourself is recognizing your own insecurities and flaws. The more you know about yourself, the more you'll understand what you're capable of handling and what work can only be done by God.

You have to come to a place where you realize the person you love is just as complicated as you are. Hopefully, they've embarked on a lifelong journey of discovering themselves and they aren't always sure what will be revealed in the process. This uncertainty can make you want to build walls that protect your spouse from seeing your wounds. As much as we want to preserve the image of being perfectly well-balanced human beings, there will be moments when life forces our brokenness to the surface. That's when love is put to the test. There's an old love song with lyrics that challenge the listeners to look beyond the sunny beautiful days of romance and truly ask themselves, "Can you stand the rain?"

Drip.

Drop.

Drip.

Drop.

Before you know it, the few sprinkles that were once scattered in your life turn into a torrential downpour and suddenly your life is flooded and there are no easy solutions. Job loss, diseases, children, promotions, weight gain, grief, insecurities, finances, time management, and sleep deprivation . . . any might create a season of uneasiness. That's what the first date can never reveal. It's not what you can see that scares you; it's what you never saw coming that can knock the wind out of you.

So how do you lay a foundation that prepares your home to withstand the winds and storms of life? It begins with understanding what values you must have in order to function in a relationship. I'm not talking about the superficial things like physical stature or material wealth that distract us from what truly matters. Storms have a tendency to change those factors anyway. This is about determining what you need for a person to have on the inside before they can connect and pour into you.

Every relationship you have, whether romantic or platonic, has taught you a necessary lesson about character traits you value.

If a relationship ended because of infidelity, the lesson it taught you was that you need someone who maintains loyalty, trust, and respect as some of his or her main principles. If everything seemed right on paper, but for some reason you and the other person couldn't click, that relationship taught you that the core of your relationship has to be friendship. My husband and I often share the lessons we've learned in our marriage with other couples. One of the aspects my husband describes is how our relationship has rooms. We are husband and wife, friends, co-parents, co-pastors, business colleagues, and hot-topic debaters. Why is it important to have so many rooms? Because when the floods of life come, one or two of those rooms may be under construction. There will be moments when friendships you've had throughout the years disappoint you, but you can look at your partner and think, *Thank God I've got a friend in you!*

Halfway through the movie, Makenzie's winter-break extravaganza caught up with her. She was out like a light. After struggling for a bit she finally found a way to turn my arms and body into the perfect mattress. She placed her arm behind my back and fell asleep hugging me. Her arm rested between my back and the chair. Each time I felt her body give in to slumber, I gently lifted my body to ease my weight from her delicate arm. But then she began to toss and turn, hugging me, and then returning her arm to the same position.

Then it hit me that I did the same thing as a child.

I used to beg my mother for a chance to sleep with her when I was little. I'd make all the promises I could until she relented;

then, while finally lying in their bed I was afraid. While I was wrapped in their tiger-print comforter and surrounded by statues of various animals from around the world—lions, leopards, elephants, and more—in my childish eyes their room looked like an actual zoo. I wasn't too afraid for an occasional overnight visit, though. I just needed my arm to be tucked underneath my mom.

I needed to know I wasn't alone. I needed her to know that her weight was grounding me, even though she feared it was hurting me.

At some point between my overnight visits in my parents' room and that evening showing of *Saving Mr. Banks* with my own children, I forgot that love doesn't care how much you weigh. I'm willing to bet I learned it the first time I had to ask for forgiveness from someone I loved. Years ago, sometime between blissful innocence and the seduction of trouble, I had to look my parents in the eyes and ask them to give me another chance. In the silence of their deliberating pause, I wondered, would they really give me a clean slate or would they say the words and keep a record? I stayed in line, I did what I was supposed to do, and things always returned to love. Conviction kept me out of a lot of trouble.

Their love found a way to bear the weight of disappointment. My love found a way to trust the power of forgiveness. Our love found a way because we gave it no other choice. No one in our family has been perfect. I'm sure if we could, we'd make a few edits to our histories, but still, through our letdowns love has always found a way. And maybe we aren't as afraid of loving someone unconditionally as we are of the possibility that they may not reciprocate.

So often we settle for becoming each other's symptom and not each other's partner: I want you to love me so I can love myself. I know a few of us have been guilty of falling in love with wanting to be loved, but merely just liking the actual person. But maybe true love is about finding the one worth hurting over.

A mother loves a child so much from conception that she's willing to hurt physically to bring that love to life. A wife is formed from a man's rib. God so loved the world that He gave His Son. All this time we've been focused on how to avoid hurt. But love is strong enough to bear the weight of the one worth hurting for. Love is not protection from pain, only strength to bear it.

Maybe we aren't as afraid of loving someone unconditionally as we are of the possibility that they may not reciprocate.

I haven't always had the patience required to let true love grow, because I was always looking for the holes where pain could seep in. Each time I found pain, I stopped watering the seeds that flourished love.

But I've come to recognize that pain is as much a part of life as air. This isn't about me being afraid anymore either. I've learned to dance around my fears. This is me realizing that love without sacrifice does not exist, so choose the one worth hurting over. Our hearts must be willing to hurt a little to make our person better.

And this is my pledge to the hearts worth hurting for:

I can't offer you perfect. I don't know the price of my future and I can't promise it won't cost you pain. I can't be certain I've confronted everything that has haunted me, but each day I learn the power of sharing my burdens with Him. I wish I could tell you I'll be careful enough to handle your brokenness, but I haven't always done the best with my own. I promise to wrap your pain with my love and give it to God. I know that He can heal the wounds you're not ready to let me see. I know He can give me grace to survive the cuts I may endure from loving you. I know this because I've given Him my best and worst, yet He still deemed me worthy of loving you. So I will love you with all of the God I have in me. I constantly strive to live a life that opens new streams for His love to flow from within me. I won't always get it right. I'll try with all my will and I still may hurt you. But I have a pledge for that:

I'm worth hurting for too.

10

Show Me How

This is not the end; in fact, it's the beginning. It's the moment that will determine how I set out to do the rest of my life. I am no longer the scared child hoping to be loved and fueled by belief. I've discovered the power of my voice. I've seen the miracle of my own resurrection from the emotions that I thought killed me. I believe there is power within me to do the unthinkable. I believe there is strength inside me waiting for the right obstacle to bring it to the forefront. I'm not afraid that I can't handle what's next. I'm excited that whatever is next is going to reveal something sweeter and more admirable about me. Life may be bitter for some, but it's sweet for me. I release my need for control and my desire to be understood. Instead, I ask that everything that is meant for me will find its way to me and everything that dares to restrict me will be removed.

My parents had been telling us for months that we should watch the remake of the 1970s miniseries *Roots*, so my husband and I purchased it on iTunes. Neither of us had seen the original, and we weren't quite sure what to expect outside of the fact that it chronicled slavery. It didn't take us long before we realized that it was so much bigger than the stories we have become accustomed to viewing regarding that time. This story was rich with the tradition of African culture before the main character, Kunta Kinte, was sold into slavery. It was engrained in him from birth that he had a responsibility to remain true to his family and culture.

After undergoing the ritual customs to become a warrior in his tribe, Kunta decided on an unusual path. He relocated to another area to further his education. His decision was met with contempt from his parents and resulted in him taking off on his horse. He was soon cornered by an opposing tribe and sold into slavery. Throughout his journey on the slave ship, he partnered with other slaves to plan an escape. Each attempt ended with casualties on both sides and resulted in no liberty for Kunta or his people. Still, he believed that his freedom was worth the risk. Time and time again throughout the series, we witness Kunta hoping to be freed from the oppression of slavery. He is sold and renamed Tobi by a family. Kunta, however, refused to answer to any other name than the one his father gave him.

There is a gut-wrenching scene when Kunta has been recaptured and brought to the plantation. The overseer seeks to send him and all of the other slaves a message that will deter any future plans they may have to escape. He ties him to the post to beat him, but before rendering his first lash he gives Kunta a chance to end it before he even begins. Kunta just had to answer one simple question: "What's your name?"

With pride in his eyes he answers: "Kunta." Immediately, the beating begins. I watched the depiction of this fictional-but-likely scenario through clenched eyes. The skin began to separate from Kunta's muscles and the muscles from his bone. The other characters tried to turn their heads but were forced to watch as he writhed with pain on a post. He breathlessly finally uttered the name his owner had given him. It felt as if he was caving into the reality that he was a slave. A part of me was saddened that he had caved, but I was also relieved that he would no longer have to endure the vicious beating.

Having reached our limit of emotional distress from watching that first episode of the four-part series, my husband and I decided to wait until the next day for part two. When we sat down to watch part two, we thought that we must have made a mistake and selected part three instead. The scene opens with Kunta running at full speed through the forest. Is that right? He was trying to escape again. It seemed ludicrous initially, but I realized that in time his wounds from the last beating healed. Eventually the pain of that moment was a distant memory, and the potential freedom outweighed the gravity of his painful past.

As long as Kunta went by the name Tobi and followed the rules of the plantation, he could live a relatively comfortable life. He may not have the freedom he desired, but he would not be beaten. Tobi would not have to worry about where his next meal was coming from or where he could safely lay his head at night. There was a level of comfort that came with going with the flow, but he was willing to dare to be uncomfortable so that he could have a life that he felt empowered to live.

While the days of that type of slavery have long ended, the enslavement of the mind is still very prevalent. We are often held captive by ideas of shame and dreams deferred. My desire is for you to dare to live a life of uncomfortableness. Outside your comfort zone there are emotions, opportunities, and memories to be made. It will require that you stretch yourself. It will force you to make calculated moves, but the idea of comfort is an illusion. It limits your ability to grow and master the art of knowing your full potential and soul. Kunta knew that if he fell into the role of Tobi that he could never fully forget what it was like to be free. Regardless of how much you try to force your mind to see your present state as comfortable, there is a version of yourself that you have not yet given up on.

You're no longer the shy teenager stalking through the halls of school wondering how you'll be received. You've survived the pressures of being accepted by peers. You're learning to cherish the moments of solitude that life carries because it is peace. You've gleaned enough wisdom to no longer have to worry how your words will land. If you simply think before you speak, the perfect answer falls from your lips. You're learning to trust your instincts without fear. You aren't obsessed with people proving you wrong, because you realize it's better for them to just show you who they are.

I pray you find the courage to be okay with getting it wrong. I hope that you stare life down and determine that regardless of what lies ahead, you'll survive. You'll learn to follow the voice of truth that has been with you every step of this journey. You'll forgive yourself for not protecting your heart in the past, but you won't allow that to create walls. You'll find the courage to be vulnerable. Armed with the wisdom of your heartbreak, you'll recognize that some people will be granted access to your universe. Their access to your heart will give them the power to do everything from excite you to disappoint you. How you respond to their actions will determine your ability to function as more than just a being, but a compassionate soul in the world. Maintaining the boundaries that keep your heart humble and pure before God may require you to let some people go. How will you know who should go and who should stay? It should be evident by their actions whether the people you desire to be in your life are willing to do the work to maintain a place in your world.

You will have peace in knowing that not many have the integrity to earn your trust because you're no longer interested in giving it away for free. You are at the beginning of something more beautiful than you even realize. A deeper level of self-intimacy will reward you with true confidence and compassion. This is not about arriving at a level of perfection, but rather understanding the beauty in constantly evolving. Whatever you do, avoid being stagnant! You are too mysterious a creature to stop learning how you can impact this world with dimensions of positivity and growth. Your wounds are someone else's lesson; we need you to teach them.

Do not compare your growth with anyone else's. The only person you are competing with is who you were yesterday. You don't have to feel intimidated by what someone else accomplishes. God will reveal in His own time and in His own pace what the next levels are for you. All you have to do is continue to leave your heart and mind open to the possibilities that anything can happen.

Fully maximizing the power of this book begins not when you close it, but when you begin to see yourself clearly because of it. It won't help if you just close it and store it wherever you keep the books that you rarely open again. This book depends on your ability to close it and begin to make plans. It's time to start making plans to sort through your traumas, victories, and dilemmas. It's time to start making plans to pray, increase your faith, and discover power you didn't even know you had. I want to help you make some of those goals before closing this book.

You need a mentor! Before you start shrinking on the inside and wondering where you'll find someone to walk you through all that is ahead of you, I challenge you to recognize that a mentor is not necessarily someone you have direct access to. Think about the people in the world far or near whom you admire. It's important to realize the only reason you admire someone is because there is something inside of you that can be developed into what you admire about them. Let go of the "if only" mentality. Your life does not have to mirror theirs for you to accomplish greatness. As a matter of fact, the reason you are drawn to them is that something inside of you is going to be birthed that complements, or exceeds, what they're currently doing.

Maybe you are not too entirely sure what your professional purpose in life is going to look like, so you're thinking that the idea of mentorship does not apply to you. I want to challenge you to dig deeper and begin to recognize the areas of your life you'd like to improve in. Through the gift of digital media we now have access to millions of people around the world. Find someone who reflects a portion of who you want to become and begin to recognize and appreciate his or her uniqueness. Mentorship is not imitating the people you're attracted to. Mentorship is observing someone's decision making so that it can influence how you see the world. You cannot be mentored by someone who is struggling in the same area as you. The person who mentors you should be accomplished in an area that you are hoping to grow in.

One of your goals must be to begin discovering mentors both near and far whose lives have inspired you. I encourage you to research their stories. Don't just choose someone based on popularity. You have to be able to answer to yourself why you've chosen this person to help you navigate through life. What have they overcome that inspires you? What have they accomplished that gives you reasons to pursue your own gifts and talents? Please recognize that not everyone who mentors you will always be readily accessible to you. But just because someone is not close to you does not mean they are not able to mentor you. True mentorship has nothing to do with the distance and everything to do with what they inspire you to believe. I often get requests to mentor someone, but because of my children and schedule, I am upfront about not always being able to offer one-on-one attention. I do, however, let them know that I have resources available online that may offer some insight into how I think and what I believe on certain subjects. Occasionally, someone at church will inspire me in such a way that I ask her to come alongside and witness my life from her perspective. It is my hope that while she is with me she will pick up on some of my knowledge and wisdom, but also that she will be able to ask questions that help me provide insight into her own life.

Occasionally God will bring someone into your life and you'll be able to glean from them. These mentors are rare jewels that should be treasured. The best way to gain and maintain access to a mentor is being clear about your objective. You cannot just take from a mentor. Your first heart should be to serve what they are doing. Through serving their life's vision, you place yourself in a position to glean from them with unprecedented access. There are many people who want to mentor, but they're afraid that a person is only connected to them because they want to imitate what they have already done. By showing your distinction and loyalty, you can begin to have a relationship with a mentor that stands the test of time.

Never stop creating goals for your life. Regardless of how much, or little, you have accomplished, there is something for you to do on earth. You cannot wander around aimlessly and think you will be able to accomplish those things. It takes extreme focus, discipline, and intentionality to overcome the many things that often stand in the way of success. When I first began public speaking, I was nervous because my delivery was nowhere near what I had become accustomed to hearing when growing up. I thought that in order to be an effective speaker, you had to yell, hoop, and holler. In other words, I thought that I would have to be my father.

One of the things that I began to do was to observe when other people took the stage. Whether they were male or female, black or white, young or old, I began to notice the way they delivered their messages. While I did not emulate any of them, this did help me to realize a few things. I learned that effectiveness has nothing to do with delivery and everything to do with the power of what you're saying.

I realized that there were other people with different styles, so my nerves began to lessen when I took the stage. I understand now my own pace and my own rhythm. It provided a level of confidence that allowed me to let the room adjust to where I was, as opposed to trying to fill the room with a persona or idea that was not authentic to who I am.

Women of Faith

There has not been an occasion that exemplifies mentorship for me like when I went on tour with an organization called Women of Faith. I was familiar with the brand of the tour, but I was not sure exactly who the women were or what their messages were. It only took an introductory meeting for me to understand what made the conference so unique. I was extremely moved by the transparency and vulnerability of the women represented on the tour. I will be honest and say that sharing my story often made me feel as though I was a lone wolf speaking about church hurt and brokenness. When I met these ladies, my perception changed immediately. Here were these remarkable women who have been touring the country for more than twenty years sharing their stories of being broken, hurt, confused, and disappointed by life. They did not allow their stories to end there, though.

As I watched them tell their stories with such strength and bravery, I knew that I was right at home. When I took the stage, I was comforted by the fact that these brave women had gone ahead of me.

True mentorship is when someone's life serves as evidence that you can survive whatever comes your way. You may need several mentors to fully touch every area of your life. You may need a mentor who reflects intimacy that you desire. You may need another mentor who reflects the relationship with God that you'd like to have. You may need another mentor who guides you through your professional career. You do not have to isolate yourself to one person for everything. Keep in mind that no mentor will be perfect, but we are not searching for perfection; we are looking for clues that will help us reveal the destiny that is inside of us.

> *True mentorship is when someone's life serves as evidence that you can survive whatever comes your way.*

What I also learned from these women is that you should never be afraid of reinventing yourself. So often we get locked inside the roles that we think we should play in order to appease other people. Above all I want for you to embrace your truth and your identity with an unapologetic strength. You cannot risk confining yourself to the roles people would prefer for you to stay in. You have the power to own your voice. Don't let people scare you out of using it!

You Are a Mentor

Right now the mere fact that you are a part of the everyday world means that someone is constantly observing you. If you have children, friends, coworkers, or family members, you can be certain that your life is under scrutiny. You are setting a precedent for someone with how you maneuver through life. Don't let your own insecurities rob others from witnessing how to turn aside from the comfort of their family culture and break the glass ceiling. You are a force to be reckoned with. Nothing has stripped you of your power. Your best days are ahead of you and you needed all of your worst days to prepare you for them. Your soul is full of promise and potential. Don't allow it to lie dormant.

You must avoid the temptation of complacency and force yourself to constantly dig within. Nothing is ever as perfect as it seems or as bad as it may appear. There's always work to be done and accomplishments worth celebrating. Don't become comfortable in your misery or blinded by your achievements. If you're still here, it's because God has something that must be done on earth that can only be done through you. You must begin to truly live your life as though you believe that. Before we part I want to share with you a letter I wrote to myself once I realized that my tomorrow held more promise than my past held pain. I offer it to you.

Dear You,

Everything you need to be beautiful, successful, incredible, blessed, trusted, respected, honored, and happy are already in your life. It may not seem like it, but only because you're focusing on the wrong things. Anything birthed prematurely risks complications. The complications you've faced that made you stop believing are simply things that you gave birth to too soon. Still, God was kind enough to teach you a lesson from that journey that made you better for His use. Don't take life into your own hands. Control the part of you that believes you know better than Him. Trust that if you don't have something it's because you aren't ready for it. Believe that if it's on your plate, you can handle it. Stop doubting your strength and testing grace. Don't do what feels right; do what makes you a better person. That may require you to have a new level of discipline or deeper level of vulnerability. There will be countless things that allow you an escape from your insecurities. Don't use them. Instead, see your insecurities for what they are: places where love can fill in the gap. Love yourself enough that the insecurities have to become beautiful.

Be patient. Once you reach the destination you have in your mind, you will see that there is still work to be done. Then you will wish that time would slow down long enough for you to enjoy the view. Find something beautiful about life every day. Look beyond the bills, the heartbreak, the dying mother, the absent father, the wild child, and the failed dreams. See the beauty in having another day, another chance. Choose to no longer worship the way things should have been. Praise God for knowing you weren't ready.

You're going to lose yourself along the way. It's inevitable. You won't always do things right, but no one else does either. No matter what they say or how beautiful their lives look from your view, we're all carrying a weight. Stop trying to see theirs; it's keeping you from seeing your own. The moment you realize that you're lost you will hide from those who know you best. Don't. You will need them to remind you who you are when you forget. Their memories of your laughter will help you find your voice.

Watch out for "they" because they'll always have something negative to say. They won't always understand why you have to be so "much." They will tell you it's because you think you're better than they are. They're going to form a clique and exclude you from it. You won't understand it, and it will make you pick yourself apart. Don't. It's not your sense of humor, your choice in music, your beliefs, or your struggles. Just be glad that you were brave enough to show your truth and have peace that it wasn't meant to be understood by them. You only want people in your life who understand that being connected to you adds "much" to them. You'll feel like an outcast, but it's okay. Great people are never fully understood, just admired.

When you start to find your true identity, people will still be looking for glimpses of the old you. Some will be unsuccessful; others will be content with learning the new and improved you. Have a memorial service for those who want to hold you to your mistakes and poor decisions. If that's all they choose to see, then they shouldn't be granted access to the blessing that is your journey.

This will be the hardest part: you're going to lose people you thought could never walk away from you. As if you were nothing, they're going to turn their back on you. You will beg and plead for a reason to apologize. You will comb through every conversation, moment, text, phone call, and encounter. You will look high and low for something that justifies being abandoned. Understand that you can only control your part. Insecurities ignored have symptoms. You can't always fix those things with your love. Leave them to God. You can love their brokenness, but only they can grant God the access to heal it. Do not think so highly of your love that you set it up against God. There are truly some storms only He can calm. A blood transfusion doesn't heal the injury; it only makes it easier to manage. When you give your love to another it should make life easier to bear. Your love may even save them from despair, but it can't save them from life's injuries. Some people are intent on hurting others, because it's easier than admitting they're hurting on the inside.

They aren't evil. They're broken. You don't have to let them break you too, though. You don't have to lose yourself trying to save them. Be strong enough to choose you.

When you stop focusing on who God is in others' lives, you'll find Him in your own. You will spend years seeing His hand on others' lives and wondering why He has yet to touch your own. He has been with you every day, as consistent as the beat of your heart. You never knew He was there because He was born with you like the hair on your head. Others could see Him from the outside looking in, but because His presence was always with you, you took it for granted. Find Him in everything you do. May every word out of your mouth be a reflection of Him. That's how you will become a light that the world cannot diffuse. When your light burns for Him the world will have to take notice.

Conclusion

I hope that this book has been an eye-opening experience for you. I truly believe that the more we understand the responsibility we have to navigate through our lives, the more empowered we are to live and dream again. As we look back in self-reflection, we better understand our need for God and can better relate with the people in our sphere of influence.

When I began writing my blog several years ago, I honestly stumbled into having a platform. I wasn't exactly sure how my life was changing in that moment, but it did. I looked up one day and everything was different.

Since the publication of my memoir, *Lost and Found*, I have toured the country sharing my story with women from all different backgrounds. I met and married my husband (I know I haven't mentioned him much throughout this book!) and birthed another daughter. I moved to Los Angeles and am now privileged and humbled to share my spiritual walk with thousands of people each Sunday.

Sometimes life can move with such a rapid pace that we fail to fully see how we have changed until the metamorphosis is complete. I did not want to have another life transition until I took the time to share with you what I've learned so far.

In many ways I felt like things just happened for me out of the blue, but I knew it was much bigger than that. By retracing my steps, I came to see that as I began to follow the still small voice Scripture speaks of, it led me to an awakening. I've discovered that growth requires a discipline to do what most cannot because they are unwilling to risk discomfort.

Growth requires a discipline to do what most cannot because they are unwilling to risk discomfort.

We stay in relationships that damage us, remain in positions that stifle us, and maintain mentalities that don't progress us. I wanted to break the strongholds that exist when we experience negativity. And to challenge women to see the good that's come from the most difficult experiences. We can allow those experiences to be the stepping-stones to our destiny.

I won't mislead you into believing this is a one-time process. We must each commit to constantly live life searching for the strength to face the vulnerabilities that make us uncomfortable. The only thing standing in your way right now is you. You're the key that opens every door assigned to you. Do whatever it takes to unleash you!

Acknowledgments

This book would not have been made possible without the divine plan of God. He orchestrated the introduction of incredible people into my life. Chief among those introductions is the man I am honored to call my husband.

Touré Thomas Roberts, when God formed you in your mother's womb, I know He took a moment to pause. How He could let an angel so incredible walk this earth is beyond me, but I thank Him every second of every day that He's allowed me to live safely in your wings. Thank you for all that you've done to create an environment where my purpose is being manifested.

I'm grateful to the stars of our universe—Ren, Teya, Malachi, Isaiah, Makenzie, and Ella. They've allowed me to fulfill my dream of being a mother. Each of you are a galaxy yet to fully be revealed. I look forward to watching as you discover what your father and I have always known: the earth is eagerly awaiting for you to manifest every good and perfect gift God's placed inside of you.

To my parents who have shielded and protected me and who continue to guide me through adulthood, thank you for the finger-prints of your love on my heart. I also have the most incredibly talented siblings on the planet. They'll probably be too busy being awesome to ever see this, so if you know any of them, please send them a picture of this. None of this would have been possible without the lessons we learned growing up together.

To Chrissy, Cammy, Cheray, Kourtney, and Rashaun: without the times we spent on Benissa, I would have never discovered the beauty of survival. You all make amazing family members, but I could have never imagined that your love would transform into a life jacket that helped me find my way home.

My name may be on the cover of the book, but there's an incredible team of people who've worked diligently to make sure that the thoughts in my head actually came to fruition. Shaniece Jones is one of them. Thank you for insisting this book become a reality and ensuring I had the time, space, and rest required to deliver.

Nena Madonia Oshman, does anyone ever tell you no? You're more than an incredible agent; you're my friend. Thank you for being an inspiration and advocate for women like me who are hop-ing to share their voice with the world.

Jessica Wong, thank you for taking a chance on my voice and dedicating the time to understand my authentic delivery. Jenny Baumgartner redefined the word editor for me. You became a covering for me when stress became overwhelming. You were the sounding board I needed and the iron that sharpened my thoughts. Heather Skelton, I am pretty sure your patience and sensitivity while I dealt with sleep deprivation have earned you a crown in heaven. Special thanks to Tiffany Sawyer, Stephanie Newton, and Jeff James for allowing me to be an integral creative partner in introducing this book to the world.

One Church Los Angeles and every soul connected to it have become such a large part of my life. I am humbled to be a part of the tapestry God has chosen to lead One LA to even greater heights.

Last, but certainly not least, to every one of you who've stopped me in airports, come to hear me speak, or left a comment on my page: You are my friends. Thank you for being a part of this experience with me. I appreciate your patience with me as I grew, and I am grateful for your commitment to coming along with me. May this book serve as a reminder that even the most broken girls can recover and become powerful women. I'm praying you discover your strength and never ever let it go.